Thomas Cook **pocket** guides

MARSEILLES

Your travelling companion since 1873

Thomas Cook

Written by Kathryn Tomasetti
Updated by Delphine Dewulf

Published by Thomas Cook Publishing
A division of Thomas Cook Tour Operations Limited
Company registration No: 3772199 England
The Thomas Cook Business Park, 9 Coningsby Road
Peterborough PE3 8SB, United Kingdom
Email: books@thomascook.com, Tel: +44 (0)1733 416477
www.thomascookpublishing.com

Produced by The Content Works Ltd
Aston Court, Kingsmead Business Park, Frederick Place
High Wycombe, Bucks HP11 1LA
www.thecontentworks.com

Series design based on an original concept by Studio 183 Limited

ISBN: 978-1-84848-281-4

First edition © 2008 Thomas Cook Publishing
This second edition © 2009 Thomas Cook Publishing
Text © Thomas Cook Publishing
Maps © Thomas Cook Publishing/PCGraphics (UK) Limited
Transport map © Communicarta Limited

Series Editor: Lucy Armstrong
Production/DTP: Steven Collins

Printed and bound in Spain by GraphyCems

Cover photography (Shop in Le Panier quarter) © Bethune Carmichael/
Lonely Planet Images

CONTENTS

SYMBOLS KEY

The following symbols are used throughout this book:

🅐 address ☎ telephone 🅦 website address 🅔 email
🕒 opening times 🅝 public transport connections 🅘 important

The following symbols are used on the maps:

i information office ▦ points of interest
✈ airport ⊙ city
✚ hospital ◯ large town
🛡 police station ○ small town
🚌 bus station ═ motorway
🚊 railway station ─ main road
Ⓜ metro ─ minor road
✝ cathedral ─ railway
❶ numbers denote featured cafés & restaurants

Hotels and restaurants are graded by approximate price as follows:
£ budget price **££** mid-range price **£££** expensive

Abbreviations used in addresses:
av.   avenue
blvd boulevard
pl.   place (square)

⏵ *Jules Cantini's monumental marble fountain graces place Castellane*

INTRODUCING
Marseilles

Introduction

Marseilles is a vibrant, bustling city. All the usual south of
France attractions are apparent – the blue skies, the beaches
with their turquoise waters and the picturesque fishing villages
– but Marseilles seems to offer its visitors so much more, and by
that we don't just mean *bouillabaisse* and *pastis*. The capital of
the Provence-Alpes-Côte d'Azur region, Marseilles is the second-
largest city in France, and enjoys a competitive rivalry with Paris.
Its 840,000 residents are spread over 111 villages within the city
limits, divided into 16 *arrondissements* (boroughs). Marseilles is the
largest port in France, the eighth-largest in the world, and much
like other buzzing seaside cities, it has an edgy, transient, all-
things-are possible feel. It's often been called the 'Gateway to the
Orient', an indication of the exotic promise it suggests as much as
a reference to its geographical location.

The city's demographics are hugely varied, with over a third
of the city ethnically Italian, a quarter French, a quarter North
African and the third-largest Jewish community in Europe.
Combine this variety with the boisterous students attending
the University of Provence and the large number of people who
come to live in the city because they've heard of its various
pleasures, and the result is an active and expanding counter-
culture. Renowned artists like Cézanne, Braque and Renoir all
painted in Marseilles at the turn of the century, but unlike the
somewhat stagnant art scene on much of the French Riviera,
Marseilles is currently experiencing a constant growth in the
arts. The city's pop music and hip-hop scene is one of the
foremost in France. Bold and defiant, Marseilles is the city that

created the French national anthem *La Marseillaise* during the country's Revolution. Marseilles is also the perfect location to use as a base to discover surrounding inland and coastal towns.

△ *Notre-Dame de la Garde protects fishermen and locals alike*

When to go

Visit Marseilles between May and July, when the mistral has tapered off and the weather is sunny yet fresh, perfect for exploring the coast and the nearby Calanques (see page 102). Summer sees the city's residents flood into the streets for festival after festival – check the Annual events (see page 10) to plan a visit during those that pique your interest. As is common in the south of France, some of Marseilles' renowned local businesses shut up shop in August, so if you're hankering after a particular meal, item or night out, be sure to check seasonal closures in advance.

SEASONS & CLIMATE

Like other towns on the Mediterranean, Marseilles' winter days (Jan & Feb), are humid and average around 12°C (54°F). Summer days (July & Aug) are hot and dry, with an average temperature of 29°C (85°F). The city is affected enormously by the mistral, or cold winds that funnel down from the Alps, so be sure to pack a light, wind-proof jacket, no matter what the season. The sun is often even hotter than it seems, so make sure you are slathered with sunscreen during the summer months, as the wind often makes the temperature seem cooler, and it's easy to get burned without realising it.

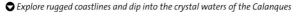

● *Explore rugged coastlines and dip into the crystal waters of the Calanques*

ANNUAL EVENTS

Marseilles has a lot to celebrate, and events take place throughout the year, with the highest concentration of festivals occurring during the warmer months. The city's most popular events focus on music and the arts.

February
Chandeleur (Candlemas) This candlelit procession at dawn, featuring a walnut statue of the Virgin Mary, Notre Dame de Confession, ends at the Saint-Victor Abbey on 2 February.
Ⓦ www.marseille-tourisme.com
Open 13 This tennis tournament, on the APT Tour, is one of the most popular events for European players. Ⓦ www.open13.org

February & March
Carnaval (Marseilles Carnival) Each of Marseilles' neighbourhoods is represented by a float in the city's themed Carnival parade, which starts on La Canebière or avenue du Prado and finishes at the Parc Borély. ❶ 04 91 55 37 95 Ⓦ www.marseille-tourisme.com

March & April
Salon des Vignerons et des Producteurs Fermiers de Marseille (French Winegrowers' and Farmers' Fair) Celebrate spring as producers from all over France gather to show off their wines, organic produce and cured meats at the Parc Chanot.
Ⓦ www.savim.eu
Russian Festival Organised by the Théâtre Toursky, performances and exhibitions are dedicated to Russian culture and the arts (see page 31).

April
SNIM (International Nautical Week) Check out the international regatta off Marseilles' shores, organised by the Société Nautique de Marseilles. ⓦ www.lanautique.com

April & May
Festival de la Musique Sacrée (Festival of Sacred Music)
Free concerts and performances take place frequently over a month-long period. ⓐ Saint-Michel Church, 1 pl. de l'Archange ⓦ www.marseille-tourisme.com

June
Ciné Plein-Air (Open-air cinema) There are outdoor showings of classic and contemporary films on cours Belsunce, cours Julien and the Panier district right through until the end of August. ⓦ www.cinetilt.org
Marseilles Pride The massive gay pride parade departs from the Parc du 26e Millénaire, and continues with an evening party of dancing and top DJs. ⓦ www.citegay.fr

July
Bastille Day (14 July) Check out the fireworks (ⓐ Vieux Port ⓛ 22.00) as well as rocking celebrations of France's national day throughout the city.
Festival International de Folklore This festival celebrates traditional customs and dance from all over the world. ⓐ Château Gombert ⓦ www.marseille-tourisme.com
Festival de Marseilles The month-long festival celebrates Marseilles and its place in all disciplines of the cultural arts, and is centred

around the Vieux Port. Ⓦ www.festivaldemarseille.com

Festival de Jazz des Cinq Continents (Five Continents Jazz Festival) This electrifying worldwide celebration of jazz attracts some of the best players on the planet. Ⓐ Palais Longchamp Ⓦ www.festival-jazz-cinq-continents.com

Mondial de la Pétanque (World Pétanque Tournament) Top international players compete for the title of world *pétanque* (*boules* to some) champion. Ⓦ www.petanque.org

Festival MIMI Hop on a boat to the Frioul Islands for live world music in the open-air auditorium (formerly the Caroline Hospital). Ⓐ Frioul Islands Ⓦ www.amicentre.biz

August
Joutes de l'Estaque (Estaque Jousting Competition) Teams battle it out to poke and prod each other into the sea at the Port de l'Estaque. Ⓐ Port de l'Estaque Ⓦ www.marseille-tourisme.com

September
La Foire (The Fair) This massive international fair has been going for over 80 years, and features arts, food, crafts and games. Ⓐ Parc Chanot Ⓦ www.foiredemarseille.com

Marsatac Possibly the largest electronic and techno music festival on the Mediterranean, this gathering attracts many international DJs. Ⓦ www.marsatac.com

October
Fiesta des Suds A festival of Mediterranean music, dancing, food and more. Ⓐ Docks des Suds, Joliette Ⓦ www.dock-des-suds.org

Marseille-Cassis Semi-Marathon For the enthusiastic (and fit) runner, this semi-marathon covers some staggering heights. ⓦ www.marseille-cassis.com

December
La Foire aux Santons (Nativity Figurine Fair) Get ready to start decking out your Nativity Scene, with inspiration from the hand-painted clay figurines at this fair. ⓐ cours d'Estienne d'Orves ⓦ www.marseille-tourisme.com

PUBLIC HOLIDAYS
Le Premier de l'An (New Year's Day) 1 Jan
Pâques (Easter) & Lundi de Pâques (Easter Monday)
4 & 5 Apr 2010, 24 & 25 Apr 2011, 8 & 9 Apr 2012
Fête du premier mai (Labour day) 1 May
Fête de la Victoire (WWII Victory day) 8 May
L'Ascencion (Ascension) 13 May 2010, 2 June 2011,
17 May 2012
La Pentecôte (Pentecost/Whit Sunday) & Lundi de Pentecôte (Whit Monday) 23 & 24 May 2010,
12 & 13 June 2011, 27 & 28 May 2012
Fête nationale (Bastille day) 14 July
Assomption (Assumption of the Blessed Virgin Mary) 15 Aug
La Toussaint (All Saints Day) 1 Nov
Jour d'armistice (Remembrance Day) 11 Nov
Noël (Christmas Day) 25 Dec

Euroméditerranée project

Never a wallflower when it comes to urban architecture, Marseilles is upping its game to an even higher level with a programme of drastic, fantastic urban regeneration that's known as the Euroméditerranée project.

This project has attracted many big-name participants. The Joliette Docks (see page 64) have been renovated by architect Eric Castaldi, and now house the offices of 300 blue-chip companies. The French container transport company CMA-CGM has been building an amazing 29-storey skyscraper designed by the unconventional 'deconstructivist' Zaha Hadid. Those who prefer more traditional architecture should reach for their smelling salts: the new 110 m (361 ft) high structure is a fantasy of curved lines and asymmetrical angles. The nearby Les Terrasses du Port will transform port buildings into shops and leisure facilities, and surrounding squares will be decked out in urban foliage. The Euromed Centre will house a Marriott hotel complex, an urban park and a multiplex cinema – the latter project led by French producer/director Luc Besson.

Architect Yves Lion is concentrating on the new Cité de la Méditerranée, which will span the seafront from Fort Saint-Jean to the new public gardens to the north, in the Arenc. The J4 pier will be renovated into the Pôle St Jean (or St Jean Centre), with an expansive esplanade and open public spaces. It will house the new Centre de la Mer (Sea Centre), and the Museum of European and Mediterranean Civilisations, which will be redesigned by Rudy Ricciotti. Like its name, the design for the museum borrows elements from a range of European cultures, facilitating their

🔵 *The Euroméditerranée renovation of the Joliette Docks (artist's impression)*

interplay with dramatic results. An IMAX cinema, an aquarium, restaurants and bars will also be opened in the Cité de la Méditerranée.

There's no point being daring if there's no-one around to be shocked, so the Gare Saint-Charles (railway station) has recently been refurbished and the Porte d'Aix area will also be redeveloped. With new high-speed TGV train links to the city, Marseilles is striding towards its goal of making visitors' eyes pop and jaws drop the very second they see the city. The Euroméditerranée project is due to be completed by 2016, by which time the Joliette will most certainly be ready for its close-up.

For more information, see Ⓦ www.euromediterranee.fr

History

Ligurian tribes were the first known residents of what is now Marseilles and the surrounding coastal areas. In 600 BC, Greek explorers from Phocaea (Asia Minor) arrived in the area. According to legend, Naan, the local Ligurian tribal chief, prepared a feast to welcome the explorers. By a quirk of fate, this feast occurred on the exact day that his gorgeous daughter, Gyptis, was to choose a husband from a pack of local suitors. Unable to resist the swarthy charms of Protis, one of the explorers, Gyptis offered him a flask of water to indicate her choice. Protis married into the family, and the happy couple received the land around the port as a wedding gift. They founded the port of Massalia, which went on to become one of the period's most important trading posts.

By the days of the Roman Empire, the city had been renamed Massilia and was the centre of Mediterranean commerce,

◗ *Explore the Parc and Palais du Pharo, Napoleon III's former residence*

prospering as the main port of trade between the Romans and central Europe. In the 12th century, ships from Marseilles ferried crusaders to the Holy Land, and it was during this time that the city adopted what is still its flag, a blue cross on a white background.

Things took a downward turn for Marseilles in the 14th century, when it was the portal through which Black Plague entered Europe, decimating the population. In 1660, King Louis XIV redeveloped the city's fortifications, allowing the urban centre to spread further south and inland. The town was a centre of resistance during the French Revolution, rallying the country with the national anthem, *La Marseillaise*. During the mid-19th century, the city's commercial port moved just around the corner to La Joliette, and in 1905, an ironwork transporter bridge was installed across the Vieux Port. Destroyed in 1947, there is now a small ferry that takes foot passengers across the port. Ever a city at the forefront of drama, King Alexander I of Yugoslavia was assassinated in Marseilles in 1934, and it was one of the first assassinations ever to be filmed. During World War II, much of the city was bombed by Nazi forces, including a huge portion of the Panier district (see page 58). The city centre was rebuilt after the war with contributions from the German and Italian governments. Marseilles has always had a high influx of immigrants, particularly in 1962 from Algeria post-independence. In the 1970s, the city was affected heavily by gangs, mafia and soaring crime levels, although this has changed significantly in recent years. With the ongoing Euroméditerranée project, many of the poorer areas of the city are being revitalised, and Marseilles is slowly becoming one of the most vivacious cities in the south of France.

Lifestyle

Although it could give a lot of other cities master-classes in relaxation, Marseilles is still a busy, buzzing, living-and-working city. Head to the markets in the morning and you'll see locals bustling off to work, stopping to gulp down a quick coffee or maybe to grab a newspaper. However, the general pace of life differs greatly when compared to Northern Europe, or even Paris. A little more time is taken, a few extra minutes are given over to a friendly exchange (pleasant behavioural traits that may be due to the warmer temperatures or the soothing effect of the nearby Mediterranean). In any case, the city's tempo provides a valuable lesson in slowing down and savouring life.

Whether you are visiting for business or pleasure, it's best to take care of errands in the morning, when businesses and markets are up and at 'em, and leave the afternoons (especially in summer) for wandering explorations or simply chilling out and watching the world go by. Family time is important, as is taking time to eat, talk and relax with loved ones. The best way to understand the city is to watch what's going on around you. Don't be afraid to chat, and if you're lucky, you may receive friendly advice or some crucial insider information.

Because of its location on the sea, and the fluctuations in immigration from all over the world, Marseilles' religious population is far from homogeneous. Most ethnically French are Catholic, but the city is also home to close to 200,000 Muslims and has a large Jewish community.

Marseilles' cost of living is lower than that of nearby Aix-en-Provence, or coastal towns in the vicinity. You can expect to pay around €1.50 to sit down with a coffee, as compared to €2.50–3.00 in other cities nearby. Hotels also reflect this price difference, with places located in the city often costing less than those in the more touristy towns in the area.

◔ *Follow the locals' lead and relax in one of the city's many parks*

Culture

The city is one of France's 'Villes d'Art' (a governmental recognition of a city's dedication to the arts) and is building new museums, cinemas and even an aquarium as part of the Euroméditerranée project (see page 14). Indeed, in September 2008 Marseilles won the contest for the title of 2013 European Capital of Culture. A myriad of cultural initiatives, events and development projects – commissioned from famous architects and intended for Euro-Mediterranean cultural institutions – are currently underway and timed to be completed by the end of 2012. For more information, see Ⓦ www.marseille-provence2013.fr.

The city is presently home to 22 museums, including the exceptional modern art collection at the Musée Cantini (see page 81), and many public monuments. Notre-Dame de la Garde, Saint-Victory Abbey and Cathédrale de la Major draw religious devotees by the thousands. Marseilles' Opera House was the second to be built in all of France. Do visit Port de l'Estaque, a fishing harbour on the north side of the city, where Cézanne, Braque, Renoir and others painted at the turn of the century, squeezing in a couple of *chichi freggi* (fried doughnuts that are an Estaque speciality) while you're there (Ⓜ Metro: 2; tram: T2 to Joliette, then bus: 35).

Marseilles boasts one of the most avant-garde scenes in France. Theatre productions at La Criée (see page 73) win awards every year and La Friche de la Belle de Mai (see page 87) is fabulous for sampling some of the city's unique offerings. Check out **FRAC**, or Fond Régional d'Art Contemporain (Ⓐ 1 pl. Francis Chirat Ⓣ 04 91 91 27 55 Ⓦ www.fracpaca.org), which organises

⬥ Visit Le Corbusier's futuristic housing complex, the Cité Radieuse

contemporary art exhibitions at their centre in the Panier district. The city is also home to some of the best French hip-hop, with local groups like IAM topping charts throughout Europe.

Get updated as to what's going on by picking up one of the free local magazines, like *Trottinette* or *What Magazine Urbain*, which are often stacked outside shops or in the tourist office.

You can take advantage of all that Marseilles has to offer with the outstanding-value *City Pass*. Costing just €20 for one day or €27 for a two-day pass, this booklet of coupons offers free entry to all the major museums in Marseilles, as well as the Château d'If (see page 62). A transport pass is also included, covering all public transport for the duration of the *City Pass*, as well as free trips on each of the city's two **Petit-Train routes** (ⓐ quai du Port ① 04 91 25 24 69 ⓦ www.petit-train-marseille.com ⓝ Metro: 1 to Vieux-Port). Alternatively, for an overview of the city's major cultural sights hop on **Le Grand Tour** (ⓐ quai du Port ① 04 91 91 05 82 ⓝ Metro: 1 to Vieux-Port; €20 two-day pass, €18 one-day pass, €8 child under 11).

● *Access quai de Rive Neuve via the passenger ferry outside the town hall*

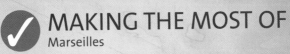

MAKING THE MOST OF
Marseilles

Shopping

The city's main shopping district spans from rue Paradis on the west side, to rue de Rome on the east, and is bordered by La Canebière on the north and place Castellane on the south. Hit these main streets and squares for well-known French and international brands like Naf Naf, Princess Tam-Tam, H&M, Kookai and Galeries Lafayette. The **Centre Bourse** shopping centre (ⓐ 17 cours Belsunce ⓦ www.centre-bourse.com ⓛ 09.30–19.30 Mon–Sat ⓝ Metro: 1 to Vieux-Port; tram: T2 to Belsunce Alcazar) also includes branches of many mainstream stores, like Habitat, Marionnaud and Body Shop.

Veer onto the smaller cross streets off rue Paradis, like rue Vacon and rue Grignan, for upscale boutiques like Cartier. Rue de la Tour has been nicknamed 'Rue de la Mode' ('Fashion Street'), and is now home to a wealth of local designers, including Empreintes du Sud. To pick up a pair of Marseilles' own 'Le Temps des Cerises' jeans, head to their flagship boutique in rue Haxo. Created in 1998, this local brand has rocketed in popularity worldwide.

Don't miss the tiny shops that line cours Julien and the narrow streets in La Plaine – they often stock offbeat wares, including an excellent selection of used books and CDs, that you won't find elsewhere in the city. The Quartier des Antiquaires, a short walk from place Castellane, often throws up an unusual gift.

Markets are everywhere, and a few of the best are the daily Fish Market on the Vieux Port, the Brocante Market on avenue du Cap Pinède (see page 68 for details to both), the Organic Market on cours Julien and the Marché des Capucins (see page 82 for both).

USEFUL SHOPPING PHRASES

What time do the shops open/close?
A quelle heure ouvrent/ferment les magasins?
Ah kehlur oovr/fehrm leh mahgazhang?

How much is this?
C'est combien?
Cey combyahng?

Can I try this on?
Puis-je essayer ceci?
Pweezh ehssayeh cerssee?

My size is ...
Ma taille (clothes)/ma pointure (shoes) est ...
Mah tie/mah pooahngtewr ay ...

I'll take this one, thank you
Je prends celui-ci/celle-ci, merci
Zher prahng serlweesi/sehlsee, mehrsee

Marseilles' local specialities include Marseilles soap, olive oil, wine, nativity figures, *pastis* and *navettes* (biscuits flavoured with orange blossom, see page 97). All of these items can be purchased at speciality stores throughout the city.

Eating & drinking

Eating and drinking are serious and passionate activities in Marseilles.

The aperitif culture is strong here. One is taken before dinner, usually between 18.00 and 20.00, and is said to 'open' the stomach, in preparation for the meal that follows. The favoured aperitif is the city's own *pastis*, an anise-flavoured alcoholic drink diluted with water that was invented either by drinks magnate Paul Ricard or by a monk. In any case, when absinthe was declared illegal in 1915, the local population was looking for a new drink to replace their favourite beverage. *Pastis* more than sufficed.

The next tier of Marseilles' culinary culture is *bouillabaisse*. Originally a fish stew made by fishermen in order to use up their market leftovers, this traditional Marseilles recipe has become a gourmet's staple. Normally a maximum of six types of fish are stewed in a tomato and saffron broth. Diners eat the soup first, with croutons and *rouille* (a garlic pimento mayonnaise), before delving into a mountain of fish, which has been sliced and dished up at the table. There are just 11 restaurants internationally (one each in Paris and Switzerland, the rest in Marseilles) that adhere to the Charte de la Bouillabaisse

PRICE CATEGORIES

Prices are per person, for an average three-course meal, excluding wine.

£ up to €30   ££ €30–50   £££ over €50

Marseillaise, an agreement as to what constitutes 'true' *bouillabaisse* – for the real deal, check that the restaurant has posted the 'Charte' indication outside.

If the thought of travelling home to a land without *bouillabaisse* fills you with dread, why not book a professional *bouillabaisse* lesson? You may not be able to purchase quite the same ingredients, but the lessons will teach you how to make this intense fish soup like a true Marseillais. Alternately, foodies

⬤ *Enjoy a* pastis *on the tiny balcony at La Caravelle (see page 71)*

A FISHY TALE
According to the Charte de la Bouillabaisse Marseillaise, the word *bouillabaisse* comes from the cooking instructions, 'quand ça bouille... abaisse (le feu)', meaning 'when it boils, lower the flame'.

can also choose to assist a gourmet chef in his restaurant for the day, shadowing the action and picking up tips and recipes. (Both can be reserved through the tourist office, €110 per person.)

Unsurprisingly, Marseilles is also home to a vast array of ethnically diverse restaurants, reflecting the population of the city itself. In particular, be sure to try the tagines and couscous served throughout the city at authentic Moroccan and Tunisian restaurants – the recipes are some of the finest you'll taste outside of North Africa.

Most restaurants are normally open for lunch from 12.00 to 14.30 and for dinner from 19.30 to 22.30, although they may serve throughout the day, or later into evening in the centre of the city. Tipping is not essential, as service is almost always included (unless stated on the menu e.g. *service non compris*). However, if you've enjoyed your meal, it's polite to leave a few euros; 10% is considered generous. At a bar, it's common courtesy to leave €0.20–0.50, or your extra change.

If you are on a tight budget, you can still sample Marseilles' delectable treats. Head to Marseilles' Produce Market (see page 98), and pick up a selection of fresh fruits and vegetables, cheeses, salami and hams. Grab a baguette or two, and if the weather's fine, take your picnic to the Parc du Pharo. Sip a glass of local wine, kick back and enjoy some of the finest views in the city.

USEFUL DINING PHRASES

I would like a table for ... people
Je voudrais une table pour ... personnes
Zher voodray ewn tabl poor ... pehrson

Waiter/waitress!
Monsieur/Mademoiselle!
M'sewr/madmwahzel!

May I have the bill, please?
L'addition, s'il vous plaît!
Laddyssyawng, sylvooplay!

Could I have it well-cooked/medium/rare please?
Je le voudrais bien cuit/à point/saignant?
Zher ler voodray beeang kwee/ah pwang/saynyang?

I am a vegetarian. Does this contain meat?
Je suis végétarien (végétarienne). Est-ce que ce plat contient de la viande?
Zher swee vehzhehtarianhg (vehzhehtarien). Essker ser plah kontyang der lah veeahngd?

Where is the toilet, please?
Où sont les toilettes, s'il vous plaît?
Oo sawng leh twahlaitt, sylvooplay?

Entertainment & nightlife

Marseilles has a well-deserved reputation for offering some of
the very best entertainment and nightlife in the south of France.
While other nearby holiday destinations, such as Cannes and
Saint-Tropez, tend to target primarily those with money to burn
and sunglasses to wear at night, Marseilles offers visitors a heady
mix of year-round concerts, theatre, bars and clubs, most of which
are easily affordable, even to those on a budget. On the right
kind of balmy night, Marseilles is fun city *numéro un*.

For films in English, try **Les Variétés**, just off La Canebière (37 rue Vincent-Scotto 08 92 68 05 97 Metro: 2; tram: T1 to Noailles, T2 to Canebière Garibaldi). Theatres like La Criée (see page 73), the **Gymnase** (4 rue Théâtre Français 04 91 24 35 24 http://spectacle.lestheatres.net Metro: 2; tram: T1 to Noailles, T2 to Canebière Garibaldi) and the **Toursky** (16 promenade Léo Ferré 0 820 300 033 www.toursky.org Metro: 2 to Bougainville; bus: 72, 89, 97) all offer exciting nights of drama, dance and music. If ballet is what really grabs you by the tutu,

◔ *Head to the vibrant cours Julien for late-night bites*

● *Marseilles is a bustling Mediterranean city at any hour*

check Ⓦ www.ballet-de-marseille.com for the local troupe's seasonal (ⓐ Various locations) calendar. Opera performances can be seen at the city's Opera House (see page 82).

The terraces surrounding the Vieux Port and place aux Huiles are ideal spots to quaff an aperitif and have a chat as the sun goes down. Most of the year, La Friche de la Belle de Mai (see page 87) organises an eclectic mix of concerts and club nights. La Plaine, and specifically the cours Julien area, tends to dominate the alternative late-night scene (which is highly alternative and frequently very late), with bars sometimes spilling out into the pedestrianised squares. In the summer, you could do a lot worse than follow the locals' lead and head down to the Prado beach area, where outdoor activities, street performers and musicians abound. Prado is a tremendously groovesome location these days. Marseilles is also renowned for its local hip-hop scene, and big names, such as IAM, have worked their way up through the urban ranks and gone on to achieve international fame. Live music of all genres is often available at bars and locales throughout the city, and there are many unforgettable gigs performed by people you've never heard of (and never will again – here, entertaining is not exclusively about forging a career).

Marseilles receives a constant boost of energy from its large and youthful student population, and much of the nightlife is geared toward this demographic, with bars closing around 01.00 and clubs often pumping wicked tunes until the wee, small hours – packing up the hot stylus at four in the morning or even dawn is far from unheard of. However, there are plenty of options for the more grown-up crowd, including cocktail bars like the Caravelle (see page 71), live jazz (see Pêle-Mêle, page 72) and loads of fine dining.

Pick up one of the free weekly newspapers, such as *What Magazine Urbain*, or check ⓦ http://marseillebynight.com for the best picks of what's currently happening in the city.

Sport & relaxation

With its prime location on the sea and a balmy climate year round, it's no wonder that Marseilles has more than its fair share of sports and outdoor activities.

SPECTATOR SPORTS

Love to watch but not so keen to participate? Catch one of local team Olympique de Marseilles' football matches at the **Stade Vélodrome** (ⓐ 3 blvd Michelet ❶ 04 91 29 14 50 ⓦ www.om.net ⓜ Metro: 2 to Rond-Point du Prado; bus: 21, 22, 23, 41S, 44, 45, 72, 83). Hardcore fans can also visit the team's museum (see page 96) or arrange a guided tour of the stadium (contact the tourist office for details). Marseilles' rugby team, Marseilles Provence XV, also plays at the Stade Vélodrome. Alternatively, head to the coast to catch one of the regattas, like the **SNIM** in April (ⓦ www.lanautique.com) or **Septembre en Mer** (ⓦ www.officedelamer.com), or check out **Les Voiles du Vieux Port** in June (ⓦ www.lesvoilesduvieuxport.com).

PARTICIPATION SPORTS

To learn to sail or enquire about fishing, contact the **Club Nautique** (ⓐ SNM Pavillon Flottant, quai de Rive-Neuve ❶ 04 91 54 32 03 ⓦ www.lanautique.com ⓜ Metro: 1 to Vieux-Port), where you can also pick up information about the 15 sailing schools along the coast. If you'd rather learn to kayak or use one to explore Marseilles' inlets, try **Kayak Attitude** (ⓦ www.kayak-marseille.fr) or **Raskas Kayak** (ⓦ www.raskas-kayak.com). There are 36 diving schools in Marseilles. Check ⓦ www.marseille-tourisme.com for a full list and information on how to organise a dive to the Red Coral Cave on the south side of the Maïre Island. Rock-climbing is hugely popular in the nearby Calanques. If you have experience, ⓦ www.topo-calanques.com contains information on the lay of the land and paths to follow.

RELAXATION

If your idea of sport tends to be somewhat less adventurous, the city offers plenty of options that are geared more toward relaxation rather than an adrenaline rush. Rent bikes at **Tandem** (ⓐ 16 av. du Parc Borély ⓣ 04 91 22 64 80 ⓝ Bus: 19, 83). Head to **Golf Borély** (ⓐ 136 av. Clôt Bey ⓣ 04 96 14 01 40 ⓝ Bus: 44) to practise your swing. Or try one of Marseilles' hammams, such as **La Bastide des Bains** (ⓐ 19 rue Sainte ⓣ 04 91 33 39 13 ⓦ www.bastide-des-bains.com ⓛ 10.00–20.00 Mon–Fri, 10.00–15.00 Sat, 09.00–18.00 Sun ⓝ Metro: 1 to Vieux-Port) or **Hammam Rafik** (ⓐ 1a rue de l'Academie ⓣ 04 91 54 21 62 ⓝ Metro: 1 to Estrangin). If the sun is shining, head to the beach instead (see page 89).

▲ Swim, sail or simply sunbathe along Marseilles' coast

Accommodation

Marseilles has a fairly wide range of hotels, although it may be difficult to find budget accommodation in the summer months or in the heart of the city centre. Try to book at least a few weeks in advance if you plan to travel to Marseilles in July or August – remember that these are the months when the French take their holidays, so the most charming places to stay may fill up quickly. Be sure to check the hotel's location carefully, as some of the cheaper options are often tucked away on poorly lit back streets near the train station; this area is undergoing a general 'smartening up', but it can still be somewhat sketchy at night. The most extravagant hotels are around the Vieux Port or along corniche John Fitzgerald Kennedy.

Lutetia £ This pretty little hotel is the city's best budget option, although a little bit of a walk from the centre's bustling action. Free Wi-Fi access. ➋ 38 allée Léon Gambetta (Vieux Port & Le Panier) ➊ 04 91 50 81 78 Ⓦ www.hotelmarseille.com Ⓝ Metro: 1 to Réformés Canebière

Alizé £–££ Directly on the Vieux Port, this hotel offers simple rooms in an 18th-century building. It's worth paying extra to

PRICE CATEGORIES
Prices are for double rooms, per night, not including breakfast.
£ up to €75   **££** €75–125   **£££** over €125

book a sea-facing room – the sunsets are divine. ⓐ 35 quai de la Fraternité (Vieux Port & Le Panier) ⓣ 04 91 33 66 97 ⓦ www.alize-hotel.com Ⓜ Metro: 1 to Vieux-Port

Le Péron £–££ Rooms individually decorated during the 1960s make this family-run hotel one of the most unusual in the city – kitsch yet stylish. Book a corner room, where you can see the sea from bed. ⓐ 119 corniche John Fitzgerald Kennedy (South of the port) ⓣ 04 91 31 01 41 ⓦ www.hotel-peron.com Ⓜ Bus: 83, 54

Saint-Louis £–££ Just off La Canebière, rooms have a Provençal country theme, with pale colours and white wood, and mattresses are of the highest quality. ⓐ 2 rue des Récolettes (Vieux Port & Le Panier) ⓣ 04 91 54 02 74 ⓦ www.hotel-st-louis.com Ⓜ Metro: 1 to Vieux-Port, 2 to Noailles

Unité d'Habitation, Hôtel Le Corbusier £–££ A monument to post-World War II design, the Unité is both futuristic and simple. Somewhat unusual and quite a distance from the city centre, this is the spot for true architecture enthusiasts. ⓐ 280 blvd Michelet (South of the port) ⓣ 04 91 16 78 00 ⓦ www.hotellecorbusier.com Ⓜ Metro: 2 to Rond-Point du Prado; bus: 21, 22, 23, 41S, 44, 45, 72, 83

Bellevue ££ Most famous for the aperitifs served at its first-floor Caravelle bar (see page 71), the Bellevue offers simple rooms on the edge of the Panier district. ⓐ 34 quai du Port (Vieux Port & Le Panier) ⓣ 04 96 17 05 40 ⓦ www.hotelbellevuemarseille.com Ⓜ Metro: 1 to Vieux-Port

Hôtel du Palais ££ The Hôtel du Palais has plain, cheerful rooms, and is centrally located, within walking distance of the Old Port and city's main shopping areas. Staff are exceptionally helpful. ⓐ 26 rue Breteuil (Vieux Port & Le Panier) ① 04 91 37 78 86 ⓦ www.hotelmarseilles.com ⓝ Metro: 1 to Estrangin; bus: 60

Le Rhul ££ One of the founding fathers of the official Charte de la Bouillabaisse Marseillaise (see page 26 or check the website, below), Le Rhul is perched on the sea, with views to die for. Sit back and watch the boats drift by. ⓐ 269 corniche John Fitzgerald Kennedy (South of the port) ① 04 91 52 01 77 ⓦ www.bouillabaissemarseille.com ⓝ Bus: 83

Mercure Beauvau Vieux Port £££ Very well located, this hotel is the oldest in the city, undergoing an entire renovation in 2004. George Sand and Chopin chose to stay here when they eloped in 1839. Very good views over the Vieux Port from the hotel's bar. ⓐ 4 rue Beauvau (Vieux Port & Le Panier) ① 04 91 54 91 00 ⓦ www.mercure.com ⓝ Metro: 1 to Vieux-Port

Le Petit Nice £££ For a weekend of total extravagance, head to Le Petit Nice. Owned by the Passedat family since 1917, the hotel has 15 sea-facing rooms spread over 2 neo-Greek villas. Dine in the gorgeous garden, swim in the heated seawater pool or make use of the free bikes to explore the city. A favourite of the very rich and famous. ⓐ anse de Maldormé, corniche John Fitzgerald Kennedy (South of the port) ① 04 91 59 25 92 ⓦ www.petitnice-passedat.com ⓝ Bus: 83

⬤ *Spoil yourself at the sumptuous Le Petit Nice*

Tonic Hôtel £££ This plush joint offers streamlined, modern rooms with internet access and flat-screen TVs. Located right on the Vieux Port. ⓐ 43 quai de la Fraternité (Vieux Port & Le Panier) ⓣ 04 91 55 67 46 ⓦ www.hotels-de-marseille.com ⓜ Metro: 1 to Vieux-Port

THE BEST OF MARSEILLES

Whether you're breezing through town on the way to another Provençal destination or dedicating days toward exploring the city, Marseilles offers activities and sights to suit all its visitors.

TOP 10 ATTRACTIONS

- **Château d'If** Take a boat trip to visit the castle that was immortalised in *The Count of Monte Cristo* (see page 62)

- **La Friche de la Belle de Mai** This is a fascinating place to catch a gig or simply meander through its winding alleys (see page 87)

- **Joliette Docks** Check out some serious (if wacky) urban regeneration here (see page 64)

- **Notre-Dame de la Garde** This wonderful cathedral (also known as 'La Bonne Mère') is not only beautiful itself: so are the views across the city that it offers (see page 93)

⬇ *Stroll the winding streets of Panier, the city's stunning medieval quarter*

- **Panier district** Stroll through the evocative lanes of the original medieval quarter of the city (see page 58)

- *Pastis* **sipping** Just the one on the Vieux Port's quayside terraces while watching the yachts drift in simply has to be done (see page 26)

- **Parc du Pharo** Grab that picnic hamper and head up to this beautiful spot which offers amazing views of the Vieux Port (see page 94)

- **Fish market** The fish market on quai de la Fraternité, often known by its former name quai des Belges, is one of the few places in the south of France where fishermen sell their morning catch (see page 68)

- **Savonnerie** A visit to one of these intriguing factories shows how Marseilles soap is produced (see page 83)

- **Savour** *bouillabaisse* Taste this local dish exactly as it's meant to be at one of the nine spots in Marseilles which adhere to the strict 'Charte de la Bouillabaisse Marseillaise' (see page 26)

Suggested itineraries

HALF-DAY: MARSEILLES IN A HURRY

Head down to the Vieux Port to check out the local fishermen
hawking their morning catch on quai de la Fraternité (see page 68),

● *Any itinerary allows time to savour an authentic* bouillabaisse

then take in modern art at the Musée Cantini or urban fashion at the Musée de la Mode, both within easy walking distance (see page 81). Finish with the city's most famous dish, *bouillabaisse*, at the Miramar (see page 72).

1 DAY: TIME TO SEE A LITTLE MORE
If you have the rest of the day free, work off that massive lunch with a hike (or take the Petit-Train) up to the Notre-Dame de la Garde (see page 93) for incredible views over the city. In the evening, head to La Caravelle (see page 71) in the Hôtel Belle-Vue, and enjoy a *pastis* on their tiny balcony. Hit the cours Julien area for dinner and a taste of local nightlife.

2–3 DAYS: TIME TO SEE MUCH MORE
If the weather is fine, take one of the frequent ferries to the Château d'If (see page 62), or spend a lazy afternoon on Les Catalans beach or the Prado seafront (see page 89). The following day, head in the other direction, wandering through the Panier district (see page 58) for an eventual exploration of the Joliette Docks (see page 64).

LONGER: ENJOYING MARSEILLES TO THE FULL
With a chunk of time at your disposal, be sure to visit the Port de l'Estaque fishing harbour, where Cézanne, Braque and other artists painted (see page 20). Alternatively, head to the Vieux Port and take a boat tour of the Calanques, or hop on the train for a day trip to Cassis (see page 102) or Aix-en-Provence (see page 114).

Something for nothing

With a little bit of planning, it's easy to have a great time in
Marseilles while spending very little money. Walk to the public
beaches, like Les Catalans, and spend the afternoon swimming
and people-watching. Or stroll along corniche John Fitzgerald
Kennedy to the seaside monuments, like the Monument aux Morts
des Armées d'Orient (see page 93) and contemporary French
artist César's Monument des Rapatriés d'Algérie (see page 93).
Explore the colourful cottages in the picturesque Vallon des
Auffes (see page 94), also within walking distance of the city
centre. The Parc du Prado attracts street performers, and
there are beautiful parks all over the city, from the Pharo,
to Longchamp, to Borely (see pages 94 & 78), each one filled
with walking paths and activities for children and adults.
For the price of a bus ticket (€1.70), catch one of the buses
departing from place Castellane for the Calanques, and
spend the day hiking in a tropical paradise.

Window shop your way down La Canebière and rue Paradis,
checking out the wares in the Quartier des Antiquaires (west of
rue de Rome and spreading south behind the Préfecture), or explore
the centuries-old squares of the Panier district. Browse through
the city's many markets, noting the seasonal produce or searching
for the perfect bargain. Visit Savonnerie de la Licorne for a
free tour of a traditional Marseilles soap factory (see page 83).
Municipal museums are free the first Sunday of every month,
while other museums, such as the contemporary exhibitions at
FRAC (see page 20) or the Musée Boutique de l'OM (see page 96)
in the Stade Vélodrome, are free all of the time. Wander around

⬤ *The picturesque port and cottages of Vallon des Auffes*

the courtyard of the Vieille Charité (see page 66), or gaze at the Jardin des Vestiges (see page 74), visible for free from the walkway between Centre Bourse and rue Barbusse. In summer you can catch free outdoor cinema at various locations. Or why not just linger for hours at a café table in the Vieux Port, watching the world go by?

When it rains

When the rain is pouring down (or the mistral is blowing so hard you can no longer stand it), Marseilles offers a huge array of indoor activities that will make you quickly forget the weather outside. Choose your area of interest and head to one of the city's many museums. Musée Cantini (see page 81) often shows free documentary films to accompany their exhibitions, so if your French is fairly fluent, sit down and enjoy the show. Alternatively, head to Les Variétés (see page 31), just off La Canebière, for films in English. For die-hard shoppers, the rain may present the perfect excuse to spend hours in the Centre Bourse shopping centre (see page 24), including the on-site branch of Galeries Lafayette. It's still possible to enjoy a tour of the city's sights from the inside of Le Grand Tour (see page 22), the sightseeing bus that departs from the Vieux Port, hopping off to explore the cavernous insides of the Notre-Dame de la Garde Cathedral (see page 93), then catching the next bus passing by. Go underground to visit the crypts in Saint Victor Abbey (see page 94), or check out what's going on at the huge La Friche de la Belle de Mai (see page 87), which is largely self-contained. If the chill is getting to your bones, visit one of the city's hammams, like La Bastide des Bains (see page 35) for a scrub and a steam, followed by a cup of fruit tea.

On a rainy evening, why not choose a cosy restaurant, and enjoy a relaxed meal and fine wine in good company? Honoré (see page 98) has a warm atmosphere, delicious tapas and an eclectic mix of items for sale in their boutique at the back; or choose one of the portside restaurants for a scalding bowl of *bouillabaisse*. The city's theatres and the Opera House (see page 82) offer a wide range of different performances throughout most of the year (except during the peak of summer), each one sheltered from the elements.

🔺 *Mosaics shimmer inside the Notre-Dame de la Garde Cathedral*

On arrival

TIME DIFFERENCE

Marseilles follows Central European Time (CET). At the end of March the clocks are put ahead one hour, then put back at the end of October.

ARRIVING

By air

Marseilles Provence Airport (☎ 04 42 14 14 14 ⓦ www.mrsairport.com) is located northwest of the city in Marignane and has all the usual facilities. There are two terminals: Terminal 1 for major carriers and Terminal 2 for low-cost airlines. Buses to Marseilles' main train station, Gare Saint-Charles, operate every 20 minutes between 05.10–00.10. A one-way ticket costs €8.50 and the journey takes about 25 minutes. For more information on airport buses, see ⓦ www.navettemarseilleaeroport.com.

Taxis are located outside the arrivals hall of Terminal 1. The journey to the city centre costs about €35–40. To book in advance, contact **Airport Taxis** (☎ 04 42 88 11 44 ⓦ www.taxis-aeroport.com).

By rail

Marseilles' main train station is **Gare Saint-Charles** (ⓐ rue Honnorat, pl. Victor Hugo ☎ 3635 (in France) or 08 92 35 35 35 ⓦ www.sncf.fr). High-speed trains link Paris to Marseilles in just under three hours and there are direct routes from here to many other major French cities. Local trains serve Aix-en-Provence, the coast and the south of France. The station is well-equipped with all the usual facilities and is convenient for the centre. Metro lines 1 and 2 also connect here.

IF YOU GET LOST, TRY ...

Excuse me, do you speak English?
Excusez-moi, vous parlez anglais?
Ekskezaymwah, voo pahrlay ahnglay?

**Excuse me, is this the right way to the port/the city centre/
the tourist office/the station/the bus station?**
Excusez-moi, c'est la bonne direction pour le vieux port/
le centre-ville/l'office de tourisme/la gare/la gare routière?
*Ekskewzaymwah, seh lah bon deerekseeawng poor leh veeuh
pohr/leh sahngtr veel/lohfeece de tooreezm/lah gahr/lah
gahr rootyair?*

Can you point to it on my map?
Pourriez-vous me le montrer sur la carte?
Pooreehvoo mer ler mawngtreh sewr lah kart?

By road
The main bus station, or **Gare Routière** (☎ 08 91 02 40 25
🌐 www.infociao.com), is located just behind the railway station
(see opposite). Various bus routes connect Marseilles to its
neighbouring cities and further afield (see page 128).

If you are driving into Marseilles from the airport or A7
motorway, take the A55 in the direction of the Vieux Port. If you're
arriving from the south, take corniche John Fitzgerald Kennedy
instead. The city is much easier to navigate on foot or by public
transport than by car, so you're best off leaving your car at one

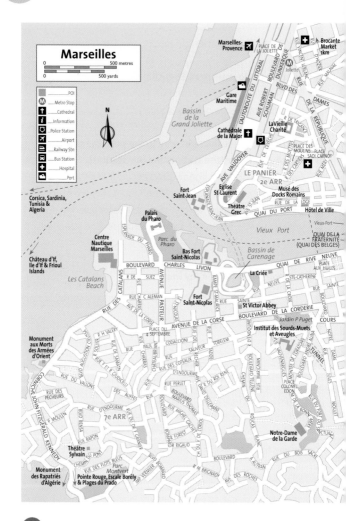

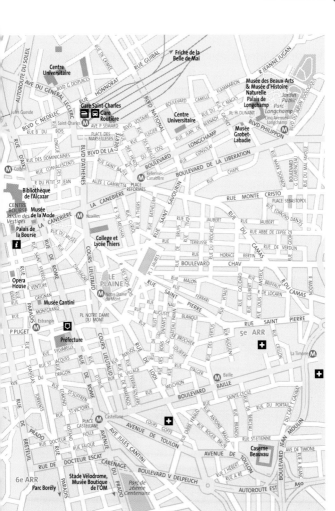

of the city car parks as soon as possible. **Parking Bourse** (ⓐ Centre Bourse, rue Reine Elisabeth ⓣ 04 91 91 19 23), **Parking De Gaulle** (ⓐ pl. du Général de Gaulle ⓣ 04 91 33 97 20) and **Parking Vieux Port** (ⓐ cours d'Estienne d'Orves ⓣ 04 91 54 34 38) are all centrally located.

By water

Ferries arrive at the **Gare Maritime** (ⓐ 61 blvd des Dames ⓣ 3260 (in France) or 08 25 88 80 88 ⓦ www.sncm.fr ⓝ Metro: 2 to Joliette) from Corsica, Sardinia, Tunisia and Algeria (see page 128). The port is within walking distance of the centre of Marseilles.

● *The new tramway makes navigation of the city even easier*

FINDING YOUR FEET

Take the time to get to know the various areas of the city.
The Marseillais are a tolerant lot so don't be shy about asking
directions. It's better to avoid quiet and poorly lit areas at night,
and always keep an eye on your belongings.

ORIENTATION

Exiting the Saint-Charles train station, the entire city is at your
feet. Head down to La Canebière, the long street leading from
east to west, directly to the Vieux Port's quai de la Fraternité,
often known by its former name, quai des Belges. The Panier
district is to the north of the port, while the Palais du Pharo
and Notre-Dame are to the south. Les Catalans beach is a
ten-minute walk from the Vieux Port, heading south along
the coast. Hop on a sightseeing bus tour or the Petit-Train
(see page 22 for details of both) to get your bearings. Walking
tours are also organised by the tourist office (see page 135).

The maps in this guide are up to date and show all the main
sights and streets in each area, but many of the places that we
list are on smaller streets. If you are planning to stay in Marseilles
for longer than a couple of days, it's a good idea to acquire
a detailed map locally.

GETTING AROUND

Marseilles' city centre and Vieux Port are easily walkable, and the
narrow roads of the Panier district are best explored on foot.

The **Marseilles Transit Authority** (RTM ⓦ www.rtm.fr) operates
bus lines covering the entire city centre and the suburbs, including
transport to nearby towns. Buses run from 05.00–21.00.

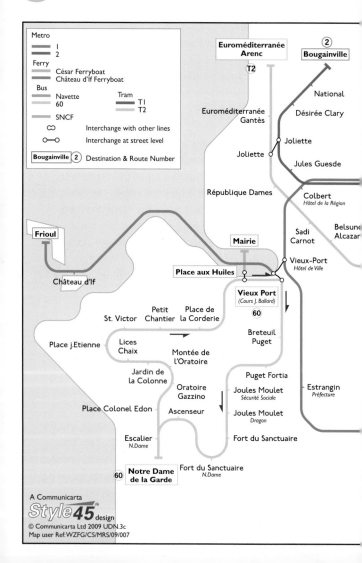

Metro
— 1
— 2

Ferry
— César Ferryboat
— Château d'If Ferryboat

Bus
— Navette
— 60

Tram
— T1
— T2

— SNCF

∞ Interchange with other lines

o—o Interchange at street level

Bougainville (2) Destination & Route Number

Euroméditerranée Arenc
T2

(2) **Bougainville**

National

Euroméditerranée Gantès

Désirée Clary

Joliette

Joliette

Jules Guesde

République Dames

Colbert
Hôtel de la Région

Belsunce
Alcazar

Sadi Carnot

Frioul

Mairie

Vieux-Port
Hôtel de Ville

Château d'If

Place aux Huiles

Vieux Port
(Cours J. Ballard)
60

Petit Chantier
Place de la Corderie

St. Victor

Breteuil Puget

Place j.Etienne

Lices Chaix

Montée de l'Oratoire

Puget Fortia

Jardin de la Colonne

Oratoire Gazzino

Joules Moulet
Sécurité Sociale

Estrangin
Préfecture

Place Colonel Edon

Ascenseur

Joules Moulet
Dragon

Fort du Sanctuaire

Escalier
N.Dame

60 **Notre Dame de la Garde**

Fort du Sanctuaire
N.Dame

A Communicarta
Style45 design
© Communicarta Ltd 2009 UDN.3c
Map user Ref:WZFG/CS/MRS/09/007

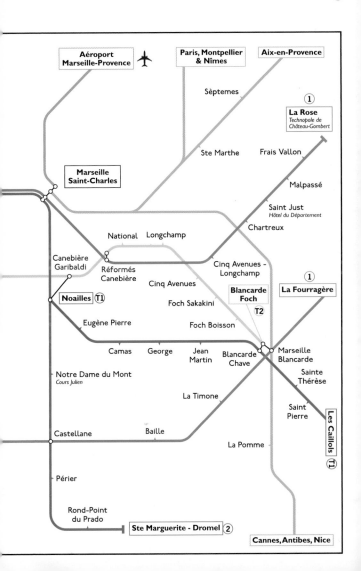

Nightbuses ('Fluobus') cover some of the routes between 21.00 and 05.00.

Marseilles has two metro lines. The newly-extended Line 1 runs from La Rose to La Fourragère. Line 2 serves Ste Marguerite-Dromel to Bougainville.

Marseilles' first tramway opened at the end of June 2007 and the city now boasts two lines: T1 (Les Caillols to Noailles) and T2 (Blancarde Foch to Euroméditerranée Arenc). For information see ⓦ www.rtm.fr.

All tickets for public transport are valid for buses, the metro or the tram. A single ticket ('Solo', €1.70) is good for one hour. A Carte Journée (€4.50) is good for one day of travel on public transport, while a seven-day pass costs €10.60. For further information about all public transport ❶ 04 91 91 92 10 ⓦ www.lepilote.com.

In the centre of the city, taxis are easy to find. Your hotel or more upmarket restaurants and bars can call a taxi for you; otherwise try **Taxi Radio Marseilles** (❶ 04 91 02 20 20).

CAR HIRE

The best spots to pick up hire cars are at the airport or at the Gare Saint-Charles. It's worth booking a car ahead of time, as on-the-spot deals are rarely deals at all.

Avis (Gare Saint-Charles) ❶ 08 20 05 05 05
Budget (Airport) ❶ 04 42 14 24 55
Hertz (Airport) ❶ 08 25 09 13 13

▶ *Marseilles' skyline stretches as far as the eye can see*

 THE CITY OF
Marseilles

Vieux Port & Le Panier

The Vieux Port (Old Port) is the historical heart of Marseilles, where the original city was born and developed. Now the second-largest pleasure harbour in Europe, restaurants and cafés line the quays, and regular ferry services depart from quai de la Fraternité to the Ile d'If and the Calanques. Le Panier, or 'the breadbasket' (named for the prolific Greek market that used to exist here), is Marseilles' medieval quarter, sitting snugly to the north of the port. A Greek temple originally graced place des Moulins, the highest hilltop in the district, and the same site was later home to 15 windmills, giving the place its name. (Two remain, but have been converted to private homes.) During World War II, Jewish families and Resistance fighters sought refuge in the quarter's unmapped streets, and parts of the district were later evacuated and bombed by the Nazis. In the 1970s Le Panier earned a name for itself as a gritty heroin den, most of which was eventually exported to the US. Over the last decade, affluent buyers have begun to snap up the charming townhouses that line the traffic-free alleys, and the quarter is slowly undergoing a massive gentrification.

SIGHTS & ATTRACTIONS

Cathédrale de la Major

Built in the 19th century, this Romano-Byzantine style cathedral was modelled on Saint Sophia Church in Istanbul. It is the largest cathedral built in France since the Middle Ages, although it's never been as popular as Marseilles' Bonne Mère (see page 93). Check with the tourist office for a schedule of the cathedral's organ

⬥ *The imposing façade of the 19th-century Cathédrale de la Major*

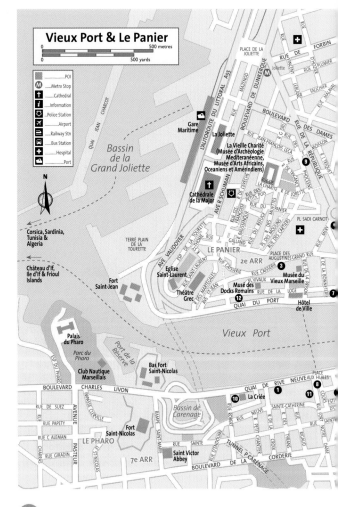

Vieux Port & Le Panier

0 — 500 metres
0 — 500 yards

........POI
Ⓜ ....Metro Stop
✝ ....Cathedral
ℹ ....Information
✚ ....Police Station
✈ ....Airport
🚆 ....Railway Stn
🚌 ....Bus Station
✚ ....Hospital
⚓ ....Port

PLACE DE LA JOLIETTE

RUE DE FORBIN

Joliette Ⓜ

Bassin de la Grand Joliette

Gare Maritime

La Joliette

La Vieille Charité
(Musée d'Archéologie
Mediteranéenne,
Musée d'Arts Africains,
Oceaniens et Amérindiens)

Cathédrale de la Major

Corsica, Sardinia,
Tunisia &
Algeria

Château d'If,
Ile d'If & Frioul
Islands

N

TERRE PLAIN
DE LA
TOURETTE

LE PANIER

2e ARR

Eglise
Saint-Laurent

Fort
Saint-Jean

Théâtre
Grec

Musé des
Docks Romains

Musée du
Vieux Marseille

Hôtel
de Ville

QUAI DU PORT

Vieux Port

Palais
du Pharo

Parc du
Pharo

Port de la
Réserve

Bas Fort
Saint-Nicolas

Club Nautique
Marseillais

BOULEVARD CHARLES LIVON

Bassin de
Carenage

QUAI DE RIVE NEUVE AUX HUILES

La Criée

RUE DE SUEZ

RUE PAPETY

RUE C. ALEMAN

RUE GIRADIN

PASTEUR

LE PHARO

Fort
Saint-Nicolas

Saint Victor
Abbey

7e ARR

BOULEVARD DE LA CARENAGE

> ### THE RHINO OF THE ILE D'IF
> Bizarrely, in 1516 the Ile d'If was temporarily home to
> a rhinoceros, a gift on its way from the King of Portugal to
> Pope Leo X. The Marseillaise were enamoured, and turned
> out in droves to admire the creature and smother it with
> love. Unfortunately, this clearly softened the little fellow
> up as it died just off the coast of Genoa, before it reached
> its final destination.

concerts. ⓐ 1 av. Robert Schuman ☎ 04 91 90 53 57 ⏱ 12.00–17.30
Tues–Sat, 09.30–17.30 Sun ⓜ Metro: 2 to Joliette; bus: 55, 83

Château d'If
In 1524 King François I built this fortress, which was used as
a prison soon after, in order to protect the city from invasion by
sea. The island and the château owe much of their international
fame to author Alexandre Dumas, who imprisoned his fictitious
character Edmond Dantès here in *The Count of Monte Cristo*.
To visit the château, hop on the 20-minute ferry from quai de la
Fraternité (€10 return). ⓐ Ile d'If ☎ 04 91 59 02 30 ⏱ 09.20–18.25
Apr–Sept; 09.20–17.50 Tues–Sun, Oct–Mar. Admission charge

Eglise Saint-Laurent
The only building left standing when Nazis evacuated and bombed
the entire district in Feb 1943, this church is now surrounded by
1950s housing blocks. ⓐ esplanade de la Tourette ☎ 04 91 90 52 87
⏱ Masses only ⓜ Bus: 55, 83

Fort Saint-Jean

Louis XIV ordered the construction of this military fort to ensure total control over Marseilles' Port. The Museum of European and Mediterranean Civilizations is due to open here in 2013.
ⓐ esplanade Saint-Jean ⓣ 04 96 13 80 90 ⓝ Bus: 55, 83

Fort Saint-Nicolas

Located between Saint-Victor Abbey and the Pharo, this was another of Louis XIV's forts, built to defend Marseilles. However, he also installed a line of canons pointed toward shore, to keep local citizens under control, as he was never entirely convinced of their loyalty. ⓝ Bus: 83

🔺 *Château d'If,* site of the fictitious *Count of Monte Cristo*

Frioul islands

Second stop on the same ferries that service the Château d'If, the Frioul islands are a popular destination for fishing or lazing on the beach. They were formerly a quarantine port and site of the Caroline Hospital. Head away from the crowds to explore the islands' natural beauty and indigenous species. The new port, which was designed in 1974, is somewhat lacking in character. ❶ 04 91 46 54 65 Ⓝ Boats to the Ile d'If and the Frioul islands depart from the Vieux Port, quai de la Fraternité

Hôtel de Ville (City Hall)

Architects Gaspard Puget and Mathieu Portal designed the Genoese-influenced City Hall located on quai du Port. For the best view of this building, take the free César ferryboat from place aux Huiles across the Vieux Port, descending in front of the City Hall. You can only visit with an official guide; ask at the tourist office for information. Ⓝ Metro: 1 to Vieux-Port; bus: 83

La Joliette

Head down rue de la République to La Joliette, the city's 19th-century hub for port activities. In 1858, Marseilles' Docks and Warehouse Company built the four brick and stone buildings known as the Joliette Docks, largest in the world at the time. The buildings were designed by Gustave Desplaces and were inspired by the London Docks. Now part of the Euroméditerranée project (see page 14), the buildings have been renovated by architect Eric Castaldi. Ⓝ Metro: 2; tram: T2 to Joliette; bus: 55, 83

---

❶ *The renovation of the Joliette Docks gives new life to the area*

○ *Archways and windows face a central courtyard at La Vieille Charité*

La Vieille Charité

Built during the 17th and 18th centuries, this enormous complex was originally a home for the ill and poor. Keeping with the style of the times, all windows faced an interior courtyard, so as not to offend passers by. Pierre Puget, the celebrated local architect, designed the courtyard's baroque Oval Chapel. Plans to raze the entire building were afoot during the 1940s, but Le Corbusier worked to get it listed as a local monument. It is currently home to two museums, and regular courses for adults, school groups and children are organised here. ⓐ 2 rue de la Charité ① 04 91 14 58 80 ⓦ www.vieille-charite-marseille.org ⓝ Metro: 2; tram: T2 to République Dames or Joliette; bus: 55, 83

CULTURE

Musée d'Archéologie Méditerranéenne (Mediterranean Archaeology Museum)

With the second-largest Egyptian collection in France (following the Louvre), this museum contains a wide variety of archaeological artefacts from Marseilles through to the Middle East. @ La Vieille Charité, 2 rue de la Charité ⏱ 11.00–18.00 Tues–Sun, June–Sept; 10.00–17.00 Tues–Sun, Oct–May Ⓜ Metro: 2; tram: T2 to République Dames or Joliette; bus: 55, 83. Admission charge

Musée d'Arts Africains, Océaniens et Amérindiens (Museum of African, Oceanic and American Indian Art)

Both a permanent collection of traditional international artworks and a temporary exhibition space, this museum also hosts rotating exhibitions from Marseilles' Musée des Beaux-Arts, which is undergoing extensive renovations. @ La Vieille Charité, 2 rue de la Charité ⏱ 11.00–18.00 Tues–Sun, June–Sept; 10.00–17.00 Tues–Sun, Oct–May Ⓜ Metro: 2; tram: T2 to République Dames or Joliette; bus: 55, 83. Admission charge

Musée des Docks Romains (Roman Docks Museum)

Items retrieved from sunken ships off Marseilles' coast are displayed alongside information relating to the city's nautical history from 600 BC to AD 400. @ pl. Vivaux ☎ 04 91 91 24 62 ⏱ 11.00–18.00 Tues–Sun, June–Sept; 10.00–17.00 Tues–Sun, Oct–May Ⓜ Metro: 1 to Vieux-Port. Admission charge

Musée du Vieux Marseille (Museum of Old Marseilles)
Temporary exhibitions give a good overview of how the city's traditions, such as the dance of the 'Balade le nez en l'air', and popular culture have developed over the centuries. ⓐ Maison Diamantée, 2 rue de la Prison ⓣ 04 91 55 28 70 ⓛ 10.00–17.00 Tues–Sun, Oct–May; 11.00–18.00 Tues–Sun, June–Sept ⓜ Metro: 1 to Vieux-Port; bus: 83, 49B. Admission charge

RETAIL THERAPY

Arterra Famous for its *Santons* (Nativity figurines), which are a Provençal tradition. ⓐ 15 rue du Petit Puits ⓣ 04 91 91 03 31 ⓦ www.santons-arterra.com ⓛ 09.00–13.00, 14.00–18.00 Mon–Fri, 10.00–13.00, 14.00–18.00 Sat ⓜ Metro: 1 to Vieux-Port; tram: T2 to Sadi-Carnot

MARSEILLES' MARKETABILITY
Marseilles is rich in market life. If you're into fresh fish, much of the produce on sale at the Fish Market on quai de la Fraternité (formerly quai des Belges) has been caught just off the coast of the nearby Calanques. For breadth of choice in a part of the city that's buzzing right now, you should head immediately for place de la Joliette's Produce Market. Antiques lovers will adore the Brocante Market at avenue du Cap Pinède where a mixture of vintage and second-hand items offer the (sometimes false) promise of a tidy little profit.

La Chocolatière du Panier The Le Ray family have been creating their own delicious chocolates according to family recipes for three generations now. ⓐ 49 rue du Petit Puits ⓣ 04 91 91 79 70 ⓛ 10.00–13.00, 14.00–18.30 Tues–Sat ⓜ Metro: 1 to Vieux-Port; tram: T2 to Sadi-Carnot

Espace Celadon Organises mosaics, ceramics and glasswork workshops and has an exhibition space where handicrafts are for sale. ⓐ 40 rue Sainte Françoise ⓣ 04 91 90 89 26 ⓦ www.atelier-celadon.com ⓛ 10.00–19.00 ⓜ Metro: 1 to Vieux-Port; bus: 83 to Hôtel de Ville

⬤ *The eccentric 1920s storefront of La Chocolatière du Panier*

TAKING A BREAK

Like any big city, Marseilles can occasionally necessitate a bit of feet-up time. The ultimately relaxed vibe on which it runs means that it's easy to find somewhere sympathetic to those who want to chill before paying the bill.

Le Bar de la Marine £ ❶ The site of Marcel Pagnol's trilogy, *Marius*, *Fanny*, and *César*, this port-side bar was also featured in the film *Love Actually*. Enjoy a *pastis* among the old photos and nautical murals. ⓐ 15 quai de Rive Neuve ⓣ 04 91 54 95 42 ⓛ 07.00–02.00 ⓝ Metro: 1 to Vieux-Port

Cafés Debout £ ❷ For outstanding freshly ground coffee and friendly service, head to Cafés Debout, in business since 1932. ⓐ 46 rue Francis-Davso ⓣ 04 91 33 00 12 ⓦ www.cafesdebout.com ⓛ 08.30–19.00 Mon–Sat ⓝ Metro: 1 to Vieux-Port

Cup of Tea £ ❸ If culture and a homely atmosphere are your thing, this place, which invites you to sip fine brews among books, will definitely be your cup of tea. ⓐ 1 rue Caisserie ⓣ 04 91 90 84 02 ⓛ 08.30–19.00 Mon–Fri, 09.30–19.00 Sat ⓝ Metro: 1 to Vieux-Port

Le Pointu £ ❹ A *pointu* is a small fishing boat typical of Marseilles. Go local by sipping an aperitif on the terrace, or tuck into their tasty snacks and local dishes. ⓐ 18 cours Honoré d'Estienne d'Orves ⓣ 04 91 55 61 55 ⓛ 08.00–02.00 ⓝ Metro: 1 to Vieux-Port

Vitalifruit £ ❺ Feed your body liquid health, in the form
of freshly-squeezed juices and smoothies, at Vitalifruit.
Stop by near closing time to pick up half-price sandwiches.
🅐 11A cours Estienne d'Orves 🕾 04 91 54 82 18 🕑 09.00–19.00
Ⓝ Metro: 1 to Vieux-Port

Café Parisien ££ ❻ Utterly French, Café Parisien is good for
breakfast or a light lunch. Alternatively, order an aperitif
and visit their *bouldrome*, or *boules* pitch (free with drink).
🅐 1 pl. Sadi Carnot 🕾 04 91 90 05 77 🕑 09.00–18.00 Mon–Wed,
09.00–02.00 Thur–Sat Ⓝ Tram: T2 to Sadi-Carnot

La Caravelle ££ ❼ Located on the first floor of the Hôtel
Belle-Vue. Go between 18.00–21.00 for plate after plate of
scrumptious (free) snacks with your drink. Décor is oh-so-French.
🅐 34 quai du Port 🕾 04 91 90 36 64 🕑 07.00–02.00 Ⓝ Metro: 1 to
Vieux-Port

AFTER DARK

RESTAURANTS
Le 504 £ ❽ Boasts the best Tunisian tagines on the Vieux
Port. 🅐 34 pl. aux Huiles 🕾 04 91 33 57 74 🕑 19.30–00.00 Mon,
11.45–14.15, 19.30–00.00 Tues–Sun Ⓝ Metro: 1 to Vieux-Port

Heng-Heng £ ❾ Utterly simple, with its long white tables and
no-frills décor, this Vietnamese restaurant is a local favourite.
Outstanding. 🅐 65 rue de la République 🕾 04 91 91 29 94
🕑 12.00–23.00 Wed–Mon Ⓝ Tram: T2 to République Dames

La Karbonade £ ⑩ Meats (including *andouillette*, or blood sausage) and grills are the speciality at this vibrant restaurant on the Vieux Port. Entrées and desserts can be ordered in *degustation* (smaller tasting) portions. ⓐ 42 quai de Rive-Neuve ⓣ 04 91 55 02 27 ⓦ www.lakarbonade.com ⓛ 12.00–14.00, 20.00–22.00 Mon–Thur, 12.00–14.00, 20.00–23.00 Fri & Sat ⓜ Metro: 1 to Vieux-Port; bus: 83

La Table du Fort ££ ⑪ A modern restaurant just around the corner from place aux Huiles, offering refined fare. The menu changes to reflect the season, but a speciality is the *foie gras* ravioli with a hibiscus-scented sauce. ⓐ 8 rue Fort-Notre-Dame ⓣ 04 91 33 97 65 ⓛ 19.00–22.00 Mon, 12.00–13.30, 19.00–22.00 Tues–Fri, 19.00–00.00 Sat ⓜ Metro: 1 to Vieux-Port; bus: 55, 57, 60, 81, 83 ⓘ Closed lunchtimes in summer

La Virgule ££ ⑫ Offers modern takes on classic 1970s dishes. ⓐ 27 rue de la Loge ⓣ 04 91 90 91 11 ⓛ 12.00–14.00, 19.30–22.00 Tues–Sat, 12.00–14.00 Sun ⓜ Metro: 1 to Vieux-Port; bus: 83

Miramar £££ ⑬ Serves the best *bouillabaisse* on the Vieux Port, at a price to match. ⓐ 12 quai du Port ⓣ 04 91 91 10 40 ⓛ 12.00–14.00, 19.00–22.00 Tues–Sat ⓜ Metro: 1 to Vieux-Port

BARS & CLUBS

Pêle-Mêle An excellent spot to stop for an aperitif, a nightcap, or to check out the awesome live jazz. ⓐ 8 pl. aux Huiles ⓣ 04 91 54 85 26 ⓛ 19.00–02.00 Tues–Sat ⓜ Metro: 1 to Vieux-Port

Le Trolleybus Music to suit everyone's taste, depending on the night. Le Trolleybus has been one of the most popular clubs in Marseilles for years. ⓐ 24 quai de Rive Neuve ❶ 04 91 54 30 45 ⓦ www.letrolley.com ⏰ 23.00–06.00 Tues–Sat Ⓜ Metro: 1 to Vieux-Port; bus: 55, 57, 60, 81, 83

ARTS & ENTERTAINMENT

La Criée Between 1975 and 1981, the city's former fish market was renovated and changed into an outstanding theatre. ⓐ 30 quai de Rive Neuve ❶ 04 91 54 70 54 ⓦ www.theatre-lacriee.com ❶ Closed Aug

🔺 *As night falls, diners begin to fill restaurant terraces in city squares*

The city centre

Marseilles' downtown area centres primarily around La Canebière, the city's central artery. Taking its name from *canebe*, or the hemp rope produced by factories that used to be located close to the shipyards, La Canebière stretches from the Réformés Canebière metro stop down to the Vieux Port. The modern tramline travels almost its entire length, providing easy access to shops and museums. While its glory is somewhat faded, La Canebière is due to be spruced up as part of the city's urban renewal project.

The enthusiastic shopper can dedicate days to this area, starting at the Porte d'Aix, heading down cours Belsunce and rue de Rome. International high-street stores, like H&M and Mango, can be found on rue Saint-Ferréol, while top designers are located on many of the smaller cross streets, like rue Grignan and rue de la Tour.

Cours Julien and La Plaine are the place to go for a dose of urban counter-culture. Stop at one of the cafés spilling out under plane trees, shop at the weekly organic market or pick up offbeat albums or books here. Restaurants span the globe with their cuisines.

SIGHTS & ATTRACTIONS

Jardin des Vestiges

These city ramparts and part of the ancient Roman port were discovered during the 1967 building of the Centre Bourse shopping centre. ☎ 04 91 90 42 22 🕐 12.00–19.00 Mon–Sat Ⓜ Metro: 1 to Vieux-Port. Admission charge

🔺 *Fountains along the pedestrianised cours Julien*

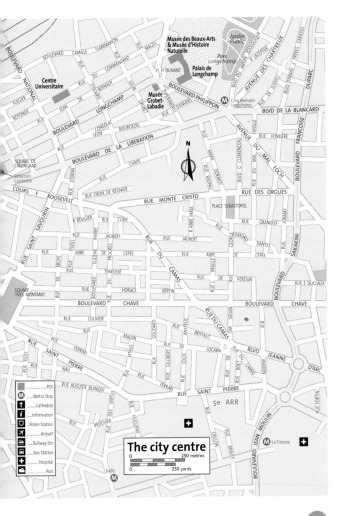

Musée des Beaux-Arts & Musée d'Histoire Naturelle

Jardin Public

Parc Longchamp

Palais de Longchamp

BOULEVARD NATIONAL

BOULEVARD CAMILLE FLAMMARION

RUE MAGES

PL H DUNANT

BLVD DU JARDIN

AVENUE DES CHARTREUX

Centre Universitaire

RUE DU COMMANDANT

RUE D'ISOARD

RUE BERNADY

RUE LOUIS

AVENUE DES CHARTREUX

BLVD DE LISSIEU

FRERES CARESSO

DUPARC

ELZEARD

JEAN

DE

LONGCHAMP

RUE

Musée Grobet-Labadie

BOULEVARD PHILIPPON

Cinq Avenues-Longchamp

BOTONDE

RUE

BOULEVARD

CONSOLAT

LEON

BOURGEOIS

RUE SYLVABELLE

RUE D'ANVERS

RUE DES ORGUES

BLVD DE LA BLANCARD

AVENUE DU MAL FOCH

FAYOLLE

RUE FONDERE

FRANCOISE

BOULEVARD

BOULEVARD DE LA LIBERATION

RUE D'ORAN

CHAPE

RUE

N

RUE MARX DORMOY

BLVD G. CLEMENCEAU

RUE DU MAL FOCH

RUE RASPAIL

SQUARE DE STALINGRAD

Réformés Canabière

COURS F ROOSEVELT

RUE CROIX DE REGNIER

RUE MONTE CRISTO

PLACE SEBASTOPOL

RUE DES ORGUES

JURAMY

RUE SAINT SAVOURIN

R ROUGIER

RUE CURIE

R ABBE FARIA

RUE

GRANOUX

SAKAKINI

RUE TIVOLI

PIERRE

JAUBERT

RUE JAUBERT

RUE ABBE

GEORGES

EDMOND

DANTES

RUE DE BROYS

ABBE

EUGENE

PROCES

L'EPEE

RUE

DE

BRAILLE

L'EPEE

BOULEVARD

RUE

DE

TERRUSSE

RUE DU

RUE ABBE

DE

VERDUN

RUE E DUCLAUX

SQUARE YVES MONTAND

RUE

RUE HORACE

BERTIN

BOULEVARD

BOULEVARD CHAVE

BOULEVARD CHAVE

RUE DU CAMAS

RUE L'OLIVIER

SEDAN

RUE

RUE

COLOMARD

ANSTRUC

BRIFFAUT

RUE DU CAMAS

RUE TILSIT

RUE SAINT

MALON

RUE DE

BLVD JEANNE

RUE

PIERRE

RUE VITALIS

LOCARN

LOUIS

BORET

NODIN

D'ARC

RUE FERRARI

RUE

RUE

DE

RUE DR

RUE FORTIN

RUE AUGUSTE BLANQUI

RUE CALIBERT

RUE FERRARI

RUE SAINT PIERRE

5e ARR

BROCHIER

VERTUS

HUGUENY

CRILLON

BOULEVARD JEAN MOULIN

RUE BRAVET

M La Timone

Baille M

The city centre

POI
M ....Metro Stop
✝ ....Cathedral
i ....Information
⊙ ....Police Station
✈ ....Airport
🚊 ....Railway Stn
🚌 ....Bus Station
✚ ....Hospital
⚓ ....Port

0   250 metres

0   250 yards

Palais de la Bourse (Stock Exchange)

Home to the oldest Chamber of Commerce in France (founded in 1599) and the Musée de la Marine et de l'Economie (Maritime and Economy Museum), the Palais de la Bourse was built and inaugurated under Napoleon III. ⓐ La Canebière ⓛ Museum 10.00–18.00 Ⓝ Metro: 1 to Vieux-Port. Admission charge

Parc et Palais de Longchamp (Longchamp Park and Palace)

This incredible structure and the surrounding gardens were built over 11 years by 5,000 workers, directed by Espérandieu and completed in the mid-19th century. The project was initiated after the drought of 1834, when it was decided that drastic means must be taken in order to ensure the safe storage of water reserves. A water tower stands at the centre of the Palais, and is flanked by the Musée des Beaux-Arts (Fine Art Museum, closed for long-term renovations) and the Musée d'Histoire Naturelle (Natural History Museum). ⓐ pl. Henri Dunant Ⓝ Metro: 1 to Cinq Avenues-Longchamp; tram: T2 to Longchamp or Cinq Avenues; bus: 81

Porte d'Aix

Built in the 19th century, this old city gate leads out of Marseilles in the direction of Aix-en-Provence. It was added to the north end of the cours Belsunce, formerly one of the city's vast carriageways. ⓐ pl. Jules Guesde Ⓝ Metro: 2 to Jules Guesde

Ⓞ *The ornate Palais de Longchamp offers amazing views over the city*

CULTURE

Bibliothèque de l'Alcazar (Alcazar Municipal Library)

Formerly a theatre and music hall where Charlie Chaplin, among many others, performed, the Bibliothèque de l'Alcazar opened as a public library in 2004, following a six-year renovation project. It currently stages exhibitions and films, and is the second-largest library in France. ⓐ 58 cours Belsunce ⓣ 04 91 55 90 00

⬤ *The ancient Jardins des Vestiges contrast with surrounding modern architecture*

Ⓦ www.bmvr.marseille.fr Ⓛ 11.00–19.00 Tues–Sat Ⓝ Tram: 2
to Belsunce Alcazar

Musée Cantini

A fantastic collection of modern and contemporary art, including
artworks by Picasso, Signac, Giacometti and Bacon, located in
a 17th-century mansion. ⓐ 19 rue Grignan Ⓣ 04 91 54 77 75
Ⓛ 10.00–17.00 Tues–Sun, Oct–May; 11.00–18.00 Tues–Sun, June–Sept
Ⓝ Metro: 1 to Estrangin; Bus: 21, 41, Admission charge

Musée Grobet-Labadie

This 19th-century family home, just opposite the Palais de
Longchamp, has been preserved in all its splendour. Wander
around the ten rooms to get a feel for turn-of-the-century
bourgeois culture. ⓐ 140 blvd Longchamp Ⓣ 04 91 62 21 82
Ⓛ 11.00–18.00 Tues–Sun, June–Sept; 10.00–17.00 Tues–Sun, Oct–May
Ⓝ Metro: 1 to Cinq Avenues-Lonchamp; tram: T2 to Longchamp
or Cinq Avenues; bus: 81

Musée d'Histoire Naturelle (Natural History Museum)

Located in a wing of the Palais de Longchamp, the Musée d'Histoire
Naturelle offers examples of worldwide species, as well as a room
dedicated to Provençal specimens. ⓐ Palais de Longchamp
Ⓣ 04 91 14 59 50 Ⓛ 11.00–18.00 Tues–Sun, June–Sept; 10.00–17.00
Tues–Sun, Oct–May Ⓝ Metro: 1 to Cinq Avenues-Lonchamp;
tram: T2 to Longchamp or Cinq Avenues; bus: 81

Musée de la Mode (Fashion Museum)

A popular museum dedicated entirely to fashion. Be sure to pick up a flyer on the way in, as it contains necessary explanations about the exhibitions. ⓐ 11 La Canebière ⓣ 04 96 17 06 00 ⓛ 11.00–18.00 Tues–Sun, June–Sept; 10.00–17.00 Tues–Sun, Oct–May ⓜ Metro: 1 to Vieux-Port. Admission charge

Opera House

Rebuilt in 1919 after a fire destroyed almost the entire original 1787 building, Marseilles' Opera House stages a vivacious selection of opera and ballet throughout the year. ⓐ 2 rue Molière ⓣ 04 91 55 14 99 ⓜ Metro: 1 to Vieux-Port

RETAIL THERAPY

Marseilles Collections Shops in the city's Antiques District sell everything from high-priced collectibles to quirky purchases. Stop by this shop for a fine mix, including old postcards, toys,

MARKETS FOR FOODIES

Those who eschew a breakfast of fried bread, sausages and chips in favour of a more healthy bowl of muesli will find that central Marseilles has two markets selling fare whose wholesome munchability will test even the most omnivorous molars. The Marché des Capucins has a fantastically wide choice of nuts, vegetables and North African specialities. On Wednesday in the cours Julien, the Organic Market will allow you to fill your basket without so much as a passing care for pesticides or freeze-drying.

GARLIC GALORE
Between mid-June and mid-July, head up to the Garlic and
Taraïettes Fair on cours Belsunce. Provençal garlic is sold
in long braids, alongside *taraïettes*, which are enamelled
clay objects.

letters and documents. ❸ 5 rue Edmond Rostand ❶ 04 91 37 59 58
🕓 10.00–12.00, 14.00–18.00 Mon–Fri, 10.00–12.00, 14.00–17.00
Sat Ⓝ Metro: 1 to Estrangin; metro: 1, 2 to Castellane

Oogie Opened by three friends from Marseilles, Oogie calls itself
a 'life store', and includes a boutique, hair salon and restaurant.
The place to shop for unusual music and art books. ❸ 55 cours
Julien ❶ 04 91 53 10 70 Ⓦ www.myspace.com/oogielifestore
🕓 Boutik: 10.00–19.00 Mon–Sat; brasserie: 08.30–19.00 Mon–Wed
& Sat, 08.30–00.00 Thur & Fri Ⓝ Metro: 2 to Notre Dame du Mont;
bus: 74

Les Pipelettes Locally designed clothes for mothers-to-be and
children. The store also stocks a fantastic range of tote bags,
printed with local maps or Russian dolls. ❸ 3 rue St Saëns
❶ 04 91 54 72 36 🕓 14.30–19.00 Mon, 10.30–14.00, 14.30–19.00
Tues–Sat Ⓝ Metro: 1 to Vieux-Port; bus: 61, 80

Savonnerie de la Licorne Owner Serge Bruna learned the art
of soap making from his grandfather, and everything in this
little factory is made according to traditional methods. Stop

in for a free tour of the site. ⓐ 34 cours Julien ⓣ 04 96 12 00 91 ⓛ 09.30–19.30 Mon–Fri, 10.00–19.30 Sat ⓝ Metro: 2 to Notre Dame du Mont; bus: 74

TAKING A BREAK

Dubble £ ❶ For soups, salads and healthy breakfast menus from €4.20 (freshly squeezed juice, coffee and a muffin) stop by Dubble. ⓐ 25 rue Sainte ⓣ 04 91 90 37 98 ⓦ www.dubble-food.com ⓛ 09.00–18.00 Mon–Sat, Sept–July ⓝ Metro: 1 to Vieux-Port; bus: 55

Eating 'pique-nique en ville' £ ❷ Pick up an outstanding sandwich or take a break from shopping to enjoy one of the freshly made salads at this cosy café. ⓐ 40 rue Montgrand ⓣ 04 91 33 76 88 ⓛ 11.00–16.00 Mon–Sat ⓝ Metro: 1 to Estrangin

Les Filles... du Soleil Gourmand £ ❸ Choose from a myriad of teas in glass canisters, or go for one of the tasty daily light snacks. The on-site store also sells quirky knick-knacks, like notebooks printed with old French travel posters. ⓐ 71 cours Julien ⓣ 04 91 92 53 76 ⓛ 10.00–19.00 Mon–Sat ⓝ Metro: 2 to Notre Dame du Mont; bus: 74

Brasserie La Folle Epoque ££ ❹ Stop for an ice cream or an aperitif under the wide umbrellas of this pavement café. Be sure to check out the old photographs and the antique copper coffee machine inside. ⓐ 10 pl. Felix Baret ⓣ 04 91 33 38 24 ⓛ 07.30–20.00 Mon–Sat ⓝ Metro: 1 to Estrangin

⬤ *While away the afternoon with a coffee in place Felix Baret*

AFTER DARK

RESTAURANTS

La Jardin d'à Côté £ ❺ A fun, inexpensive spot favoured by Marseilles' young crowd. Try the *Assiette Marseillaise* (Marseilles plate) for a little taste of their specialities. ⓐ 65 cours Julien ⓣ 04 91 94 15 51 ⓛ 11.30–15.00, 19.30–22.30 Mon–Sat, June–Sept; 11.30–15.00, 19.30–22.30 Mon–Fri, 11.30–15.00 Sat, Oct–May ⓜ Metro: 2 to Notre Dame du Mont; bus: 74

Le Carbone ££ ❻ Enjoy French cuisine with Asian highlights, while listening to jazzy music and checking out the retro décor. At lunch, try the excellent value €16 menu. ⓐ 22 rue Sainte ⓣ 04 91 55 52 73 ⓛ 12.00–14.30, 20.00–23.00 Mon–Sat, Sept–July ⓜ Metro: 1 to Vieux-Port; bus: 55

La Patte de l'Ours ££ ❼ With a menu favouring organic produce and based entirely on seasonal specialties, this little gem is a fine balance between upmarket restaurant and healthy cuisine. Finish off your meal with one of their fabulous international coffee blends. ⓐ 4 pl. Cézanne ⓣ 09 54 80 39 21 ⓛ 10.00–17.00 Wed & Sun, 10.00–00.00 Thur–Sat ⓜ Metro: 2 to Notre Dame du Mont; bus: 74

Le Resto Provençal ££ ❽ The funky décor and checkerboard floors set the stage for tasty recipes from the region. ⓐ 64 cours Julien ⓣ 04 91 48 85 12 ⓛ 12.00–14.00 Tues–Fri, 20.00–22.30 Tues–Sat ⓜ Metro: 2 to Notre Dame du Mont; bus: 74

Toinou Coquillages ££ ❾ A Marseilles institution, this seafood spot has been in business for over 40 years. Fancy oysters on the beach? Buy seafood to take away from their stand too. ⓐ 18 cours St Louis, off La Canebière ⓣ 04 91 54 08 79 ⓦ www.toinou.com ⓛ 11.30–22.00 Mon–Sat, 11.30–14.00, 18.00–22.00 Sun ⓝ Metro: 2; tram: T1 to Noailles

BARS & CLUBS
New Cancan One of the most popular gay clubs in Marseilles. ⓐ 3–7 rue Sénac de Meilhan ⓣ 04 91 48 59 76 ⓦ www.newcancan.com ⓛ 23.00–dawn Thur–Sun ⓝ Metro: 2; tram: T1 to Noailles

ARTS & ENTERTAINMENT
Espace Julien For theatre, comedy and live music, check out the weekly happenings at Espace Julien. ⓐ 39 cours Julien ⓣ 04 91 24 34 10 ⓦ www.espace-julien.com ⓝ Metro: 2 to Notre Dame du Mont; bus: 74

La Friche de la Belle de Mai Located in a former tobacco factory, La Friche stages everything from exhibitions and theatre to gastronomic events and concerts. Constantly in flux, days could be whiled away in this massive complex. It's located on the outskirts of the city centre, to the left off rue Guibal. ⓐ 41 rue Jobin ⓣ 04 95 04 95 04 ⓦ www.lafriche.org ⓛ Mostly closed in Aug ⓝ Bus: 33, 34, 49

THE CITY

South of the port

Marseilles sprawls southward from the Vieux Port. Neighbourhoods fluctuate from the tangle of streets just behind quai de Rive Neuve to the spacious avenue du Prado. An eclectic mix of restaurants, beaches and business centres, this area of Marseilles is the city's most varied, and is an appropriate reflection of its many facets.

SIGHTS & ATTRACTIONS

Avenue du Prado
Often called Marseilles' Champs-Elysées, the avenue du Prado is home to boutiques and business centres, while large shady trees spread over the daily market. Visit place Castellane, with its famous

marble fountain built and donated to the city by Jules Cantini,
and the Parc du 26ème Centaire (the 26th Century Park, also
known as the Millennium Park). The latter was inaugurated in
2000 to celebrate the city's 2,600 years of history, and includes
26 sequoias (one for each century). ● Park: 08.00–21.00 May–Aug;
08.00–19.00 Mar & Apr, Sept & Oct; 08.00–17.30 Nov–Feb
⊛ Metro: 1, 2 to Castellane, then bus: 18, 42, 50

Beaches
Public and private beaches line the coast, from **Les Catalans**
(⊛ Bus: 83), to the Prado beaches, created using land reclaimed
from the building of the city's metro system in the 1970s, down
to the **Pointe Rouge** (⊛ Bus: 19). Near the Parc du Prado, there is

● *The sand and shallow waters at Les Catalans beach are perfect for kids*

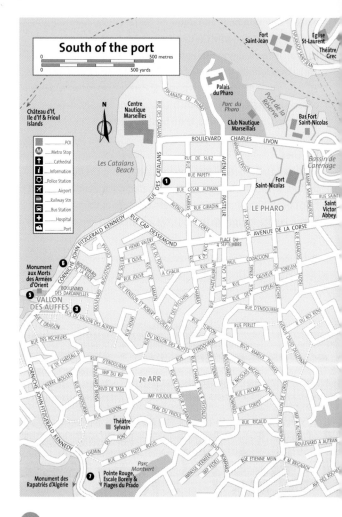

South of the port

0 — 500 metres
0 — 500 yards

Château d'If, Ile d'If & Frioul Islands

Centre Nautique Marseilles

Fort Saint-Jean

Eglise St-Laurent

Théâtre/ Grec

Palais du Pharo

Parc du Pharo

Port de la Reserve

Bas Fort Saint-Nicolas

Club Nautique Marseillais

POI
M — Metro Stop
✝ — Cathedral
ℹ — Information
🚓 — Police Station
✈ — Airport
🚉 — Railway Stn
🚌 — Bus Station
➕ — Hospital
⚓ — Port

Les Catalans Beach

Bassin de Carénage

BOULEVARD CHARLES LIVON

RUE DES CATALANS

ESPLANADE DU PHARO

RUE DE SUEZ

AVENUE PASTEUR

RUE PAPETY

Fort Saint-Nicolas

RUE CÉSAR ALEMAN

LE PHARO

RUE GIRADIN

AVENUE DE LA CORSE

Saint Victor Abbey

RUE CAP DESSEMOND

AVENUE DE LA CORSE

RUE HENRI VALERY

RUE DU TOUR

PLACE DU 4 SEPTEMBRE

Monument aux Morts des Armées d'Orient

CORNICHE JOHN FITZGERALD KENNEDY

BOULEVARD DE LA BAIE

BOULEVARD DES DARDANELLES

VALLON DES AUFFES

RUE DU VALLON DES AUFFES

RUE D'ENDOURME

7e ARR

RUE D'ENDOURME

Théâtre Sylvain

Parc Montvert

Monument des Rapatriés d'Algérie

Pointe Rouge, Escale Borely & Plages du Prado

CORNICHE JOHN FITZGERALD KENNEDY

BOULEVARD AUTRAN

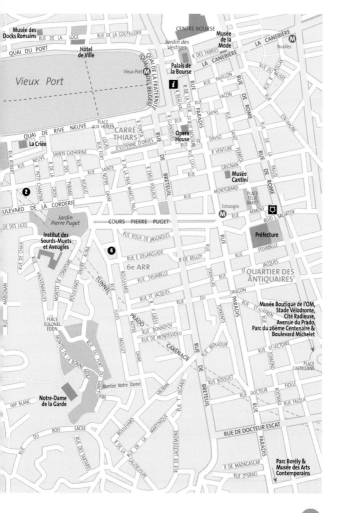

one beach reserved solely for the use of windsurfers. Public beaches tend to be crowded – if you need a little more space, try La Paillote des Catalans (next door to Les Catalans). Entrance for the day is just €5.

Carré Thiars

Located just south of the Vieux Port and north of rue Sainte, this area was originally built by Louis XIV in order to house an arsenal of galleys. The project was never fully realised, and the abandoned warehouses and courtyards have now been taken over by a lively variety of restaurants, bars, galleries and theatres.
🔵 Metro: 1 to Vieux-Port

Cité Radieuse

This 'Radiant City' was designed by Swiss architect Charles-Edouard Jeanneret (Le Corbusier), and built between 1947 and 1952. Raoul Dautry, the city's post-war Minister of Reconstruction, employed Le Corbusier to assist in solving massive housing shortages. The result was this incredible futuristic housing complex, made up of 338 apartments on 18 floors. 🅐 280 blvd Michelet 🔵 04 91 16 78 00

> **IF YOU FANCY A LONG SIT DOWN...**
> According to the Guinness Book of World Records, the bench located on corniche John Fitzgerald Kennedy is longest in the world! Take bus 83 over from quai de la Fraternité (formerly quai des Belges) in order to check it out and be enthralled by the fine sea views.

Ⓝ Metro: 2 to Rond-Point du Prado; bus: 21, 22, 23, 41S, 44, 45, 72, 83; shuttle bus from Gare Saint-Charles

Monument aux Morts des Armées d'Orient

The sculptor Sartorio created this monument, dedicated to fallen soldiers. Perfectly positioned on the corniche John Fitzgerald Kennedy, visitors standing in front of the sculpture have a direct view of the Château d'If. Ⓝ Bus: 83

Monument des Rapatriés d'Algérie

Created by the contemporary artist César, this sculpture honours those who chose to settle in Marseilles after Algerian independence. ⓐ corniche John Fitzgerald Kennedy Ⓝ Bus: 83

Notre-Dame de la Garde ('La Bonne Mère')

The moment you arrive in Marseilles, this striking landmark will be one of the first things to catch your gaze. Originally a 13th-century chapel, the prime location of the Notre-Dame de la Garde led François I to enlarge and fortify the church, for the protection of the city, during the 16th century. Modified and tweaked over the years, the enormous Romanesque-Byzantine basilica was completed by Espérandieu in the 19th century. The Notre-Dame de la Garde and its 10 m (33 ft) high Virgin Mary (La Bonne Mère), are believed to protect local fishermen, and a procession to the church is made every 15 August. ⓐ pl. Colonel Edon ❶ 04 91 13 40 80 Ⓦ www.notredamedelagarde.com ❶ 07.00–19.00 June–Sept; 07.30–17.30 Oct–May Ⓝ Bus: 60 (also accessible by foot, Petit-Train and Le Grand Tour bus)

Parc et Palais du Pharo (Pharo Park & Palace)

Formerly Napoleon III's local imperial residence, this majestic
building and its surrounding gardens offer some of the most
spectacular views in the entire city. Be sure to circle around
to check out the seascapes and views to the nearby islands.
Conferences are now held in the palace, and the park is open
daily. ⓐ 58 blvd Charles Livon ⓛ Park: 09.00–22.00 Ⓝ Bus: 81, 83

Saint Victor Abbey

With foundations that date from the fifth century, the Saint
Victor Abbey was renovated and rebuilt in the 13th century
after barbarian invasions. Visit the extensive underground
crypts, where the walnut statue Notre Dame de Confession
(commonly referred to as the Black Virgin) is housed.
Thousands of pilgrims flock to the Abbey for the yearly
Candlemas celebrations (see page 10). ⓐ 3 rue de l'Abbaye,
off rue Sainte ⓣ 04 96 11 22 60 ⓛ 09.00–19.00 Ⓝ Metro: 1
to Vieux-Port. Admission charge for crypts

Vallon des Auffes

Take a stroll down to this picturesque fishing port, where brightly
coloured cottages are interspersed with a range of excellent
restaurants. Ⓝ Bus: 83

CULTURE

Musée des Arts Contemporains (Contemporary Art Museum)

Cutting-edge contemporary artworks exhibited in a verdant
setting. ⓐ 69 blvd d'Haifa ⓣ 04 91 25 01 07 ⓛ 10.00–17.00 Tues–Sun,

🔺 *Peaceful Vallon des Auffes offers a welcome break from the city's bustle*

Oct–May; 11.00–18.00 Tues–Sun, June–Sept Métro: Rond-Point
du Prado; bus: 23, 45, 69. Admission charge

Musée Boutique de l'OM (Olympique Marseilles Football Museum)
If football's your passion, check out this little museum dedicated
to the local Marseilles team. ⓐ blvd Michelet, Vélodrome Stadium
🕐 10.00–19.00 Mon–Sat, June–Sept; 10.00–13.00, 14.00–18.00
Mon–Sat, Oct–May 🔵 Metro: 2 to Rond-Point du Prado; bus: 21

RETAIL THERAPY

Les Arcenaulx Part restaurant, part library and a bookshop
selling rare, out-of-print publications about Marseilles and its
culture, gastronomy and people. ⓐ 25 cours d'Estienne d'Orves

🔽 *Try the original orange-blossom biscuits at their birthplace*

MARSEILLES' OLDEST AUTHENTICATED BISCUIT
Biscuit dating is a science that its practitioners find to be fraught with inexactitude, yet there is one item on whose nativity everyone can agree, and that is that the *navette* was born in 1781 in Marseilles in the shop now called the Four des Navettes. Navettes are sweet biscuits flavoured with the extract of orange blossom, and they are formed (roughly) to the shape of rowing boats. Why this should be is the subject for enough debate to make us conclude that nobody really knows. The Four des Navettes is still going strong on the back of them, and does a roaring trade in the basic model and all the variations that have evolved over the years; quite intriguingly, it retains – and uses – the very same oven in which the very first batch of blossom-flavoured beauties was produced.
Four des Navettes ⓐ 136 rue Sainte
ⓦ www.fourdesnavettes.com ⓒ 07.00–20.00 Mon–Sat, 09.00–13.00, 15.00–19.30 Sun, Sept–July; 09.00–13.00, 15.00–19.30 Aug ⓝ Metro: 1 to Vieux-Port; bus: 54, 81, 83

ⓣ 04 91 59 80 37 ⓦ www.jeanne-laffitte.com ⓒ 10.00–19.00 Tues–Sat ⓝ Metro: 1 to Vieux-Port

Sugar Despite the name, this chic shop sells not confectionery but clothing creations by one of Marseilles' up-and-coming young designers. ⓐ 16 rue Lulli ⓣ 04 91 33 47 52 ⓦ www.sugarproduct.com ⓒ 10.00–19.00 Mon–Sat ⓝ Metro: 1 to Vieux-Port

---

MARKETS

The markets of this area are special in that they sell products that have often come straight down from the port – and so have the witticisms that pour from the stall-owners.

Produce Market ⓐ pl. Castellane (odd-numbered side)
🕑 08.00–13.00 Mon–Sat , Metro: 1, 2 to Castellane; 2 to Périer
Flower Market ⓐ pl. Castellane (even-numbered side)
🕑 08.00–13.00 Fri Ⓝ Metro: 1, 2 to Castellane; 2 to Périer

Temps des Cerises Boutique Hankering after a pair of these made-in-Marseilles jeans? Head to their boutique, located just off avenue du Prado. ⓐ 9 rue Haxo ❶ 04 91 33 97 78 ⓦ www.letempsdescerisesjeans.com 🕑 10.00–19.00 Mon–Sat Ⓝ Metro: 2 to Rond-Point du Prado; bus: 19, 21, 41S, 73, 74

TAKING A BREAK

Les Akolytes £ ❶ A modern, brightly coloured spot for cool drinks and light snacks, across the street from Les Catalans beach. To try the mix of ethnic dishes, order the €19 menu, which includes four tapas and two desserts. ⓐ 41 rue Papety ❶ 04 91 59 17 10 🕑 12.00–14.30, 20.00–00.00 Mon–Fri, 20.00–00.00 Sat Ⓝ Bus: 83

Honoré ££ ❷ Combo restaurant with a boutique in the back, owner Annick designs items like embroidered bags, while the restaurant serves up tapas and light meals. ⓐ 121 rue Sainte

ℹ 04 91 33 08 34 🌐 www.honore-france.com 🕐 Restaurant: lunch
Tues–Fri, dinner Thur–Sat (times vary); boutique: 10.00–19.00
Tues–Sat 🚇 Metro: 1 to Vieux-Port; bus: 54, 81, 83

AFTER DARK

RESTAURANTS

Chez Fonfon ££ ❸ Reputedly a favourite spot of Sean Connery,
Chez Fonfon was also featured in the film *The French Connection*
(Fernando Rey stops here). The modern French cuisine includes
reasonably priced *bouillabaisse* in an unbelievably cute location.
📍 14 rue du Vallon des Auffes ℹ 04 91 52 14 38 🌐 www.chez-
fonfon.com 🕐 12.00–13.45 Tues–Sat, 19.00–21.45 Mon–Sat 🚍 Bus: 83

Sushi Street Café ££ ❹ Bizarrely set up by an Irishman in
Marseilles, this little spot serves up the best sushi in the city.
📍 24 blvd Notre-Dame ℹ 04 91 54 17 90 🕐 Lunch Tues–Fri,
dinner Tues–Sat (times vary) 🚍 Bus: 57

L'Epuisette £££ ❺ Just off rue du Vallon des Auffes, L'Epuisette's
terrace is almost directly at sea level. One of the most romantic
places around, and outstanding food too, such as cod infused
with scallops' eggs and truffles. Michelin-starred. 📍 156 rue
du Vallon des Auffes ℹ 04 91 52 17 82 🌐 www.l-epuisette.com
🕐 12.15–13.30, 19.30–21.30 Tues–Sat, Sept–July 🚍 Bus: 83

Le Peron £££ ❻ With a beautiful teak terrace, views over the sea
and Ile d'If, you may almost forget that this joint is Michelin-starred
– until you taste the high-end entrées like red tuna in satay and

⬥ *Sea views and sunshine on the terrace of Le Peron*

see the extensive wine list. ⓐ 59 corniche John Fitzgerald Kennedy
ⓘ 04 91 52 15 22 ⓛ 12.00–14.00, 20.00–22.00 ⓝ Bus: 83

Le Rhul £££ ❼ As one would expect from a founding member of the
'Charte de la Bouillabaisse Marseillaise' (see page 26), the excellent
bouillabaisse at this seaside locale is apparently favoured by Jacques
Chirac and the Rolling Stones. ⓐ 269 corniche John Fitzgerald
Kennedy ⓘ 04 91 52 01 77 ⓦ www.bouillabaissemarseille.com
ⓛ 12.00–14.00, 19.30–22.00 ⓝ Bus: 83

BARS & CLUBS
Escale Borély This large waterfront complex houses a wide range
of bars, cafés and restaurants. For a trendy take on karaoke, or club
nights aimed at a youthful crowd, choose the Café de la Plage.
ⓐ 142 av. Pierre Mendès France ⓝ Bus: 83

⬦ *Traditional wooden fishing boats line the Cassis harbour*

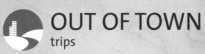

OUT OF TOWN
trips

OUT OF TOWN

Cassis & the Calanques

The town of Cassis is a beautiful little fishing village. Although
it now earns a living primarily from tourism and its famous AOC
(Appellation d'Origine Contrôlée) wine, Cassis' original claim to
fame was as an important quarry: the stone quays in Marseilles'
Vieux Port come from here (as does the base of the US's Statue
of Liberty). The Massif des Calanques, 20 km (12 miles) of rocky
coves and cliffs located between Marseilles and Cassis, is really
only accessible by boat or on foot. Visiting it can be as adventurous
as you wish: there are easy walks in from both ends, or you can
scale the heights with radical rock-climbing. Be sure to check
for seasonal closures, implemented to prevent forest fires when
weather is very dry. Call ☏ 08 11 20 13 13 or check with the tourist
office for further information.

GETTING THERE

By rail
Cassis is located 22 km (14½ miles) from Marseilles' city centre.
Trains between the two cities run four to five times per hour,
from 06.00–23.05 (direction Cassis), and from 05.15–22.10
(direction Marseilles). The journey lasts about 30 minutes.
For timetables, call 3635 or see ⓦ www.ter-sncf.fr. Cassis train
station is located 3.5 km (just over 2 miles) outside the city
centre and has plenty of buses (Mon–Sat) and taxis. The
Calanques cannot be accessed directly by train.

⏵ *Rugged cliffs provide shelter in the secluded bay of the Calanque d'En Vau*

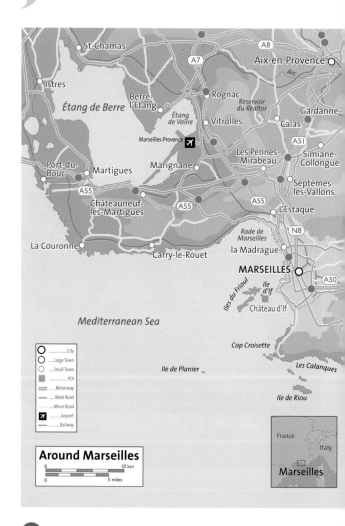

St-Chamas

Istres

A8

A7

Aix-en-Provence

Arc

Berre-l'Étang

Étang de Berre

Rognac

Reservoir du Réaltor

Gardanne

Étang de Vaine

Vitrolles

Calas

Marseilles-Provence ✈

A51

Les Pennes-Mirabeau

Simiane-Collongue

Port-du-Bouc

Martigues

Marignane

Septèmes-les-Vallons

A55

Châteauneuf-les-Martigues

A55

A55

L'Estaque

La Couronne

Carry-le-Rouet

Rade de Marseilles

N8

la Madrague

MARSEILLES

A50

Îles du Frioul

Île d'If

Château d'If

Mediterranean Sea

Cap Croisette

Les Calanques

Île de Planier

Île de Riou

O ....City
O ....Large Town
O ....Small Town
■ ....POI
▬ ....Motorway
▬ ....Main Road
....Minor Road
✈ ....Airport
▬ ....Railway

Around Marseilles

0   10 km
0   5 miles

France

Italy

Marseilles

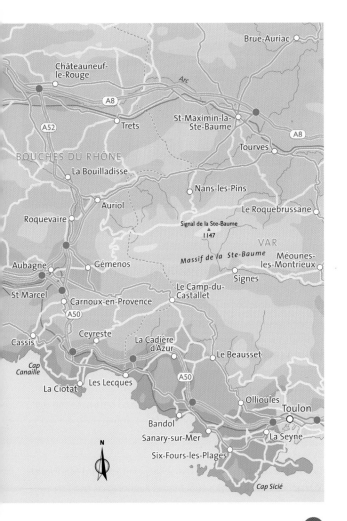

Brue-Auriac

Châteauneuf-le-Rouge

Arc

A8

A52

Trets

St-Maximin-la-Ste-Baume

A8

Tourves

BOUCHES DU RHÔNE

La Bouilladisse

Nans-les-Pins

Auriol

Le Roquebrussane

Roquevaire

Signal de la Ste-Baume
▲ 1147

VAR

Massif de la Ste-Baume

Méounes-les-Montrieux

Aubagne

Gémenos

Signes

St Marcel

Le Camp-du-Castellet

Carnoux-en-Provence

A50

Cassis

Ceyreste

La Cadière d'Azur

Le Beausset

Cap Canaille

La Ciotat

Les Lecques

A50

Ollioules

Toulon

Bandol

Sanary-sur-Mer

La Seyne

Six-Fours-les-Plages

N

Cap Sicié

● *Pastel colours and fragrant flowers at Cassis' train station*

By road

Buses depart directly for Cassis via the motorway from
place Castellane (🚌 Bus: M6, three times per day via motorway
🌐 www.lepilote.com). The fastest way to drive to Cassis is on the
A50. Alternatively, take the scenic route by heading out of Marseilles
through the Prado area and boulevard Michelet. Follow the signs
for Cassis along the D559, or stop anywhere along the way to visit
the Calanques of Callelongue, Sormiou and Morgiou. Once you've
arrived at Cassis, park just outside the town centre at Parking
Gorguettes (free) and take the shuttle (€0.50 return) to the main
square. Other (paying) car parks are dotted around the town centre.

By water

To visit the Calanques from Marseilles, contact **Icard Maritime/
Marseilles Côté Mer** (📍 1 quai Marcel Pagnol 📞 04 91 33 03 29

www.marseille-cote-mer.com). To visit the Calanques from Cassis, contact **Les Bateliers Cassidains** (☎ 04 42 01 90 83 ⓦ www.calanques-cassis.com) or head to the yellow hut on quai Saint-Pierre for daily schedules and tickets. Excursions depart approximately every 30 minutes, visiting three-to-eight Calanques by sea. During the summer, you can also choose to get off at the Calanque d'En Vau. Spend the morning enjoying the gorgeous beach, then hike your way back to Cassis (two hours, moderately difficult).

CASSIS

SIGHTS & ATTRACTIONS

Cassis' AOC (Appellation d'Origine Contrôlée) wines are some of France's most celebrated. The **local tourist office** (ⓐ quai des Moulins ☎ 08 92 25 98 92) has information on the 'Vin et Terroir' walk, a stroll through the vineyards that surround the town. Alternatively, contact **Syndicat des Vignerons de Cassis** (ⓐ Château de Fontcreuse, 13 route de La Ciotat ☎ 04 42 01 71 09) to arrange to view one of the 12 *domaines* nearby. Particularly recommended is Domaine du Paternel's Cassis Blanc, an outstanding wine. Wines from

APPELLATION D'ORIGINE CONTROLEE

AOC is nothing more fancy than a quality assurance guarantee. It signifies that a wine has been produced to a standard of soil, climate and grape conditions, but – please note – it makes no promises about the quality of the wine itself.

Clos Sainte-Madeline are popular, as are those from the Domaine des Quatre Vents, particularly the rosés.

CULTURE
Fondation Camargo
Formerly the Hôtel Panorama, in 1967 this was purchased by American artist Jerome Hill, and he commenced his residency programme for artists, composers and scholars here. Concerts and lectures, often in English, are held frequently, as is the annual Printemps du Livre. ⓐ av. de l'Amiral Ganteaume ⓣ 04 42 01 11 57 ⓦ www.camargofoundation.org, www.printempsdulivre-cassis.org

Musée Méditerranéen d'Art et Traditions Populaires
For a dose of Provençal artworks and artefacts, head to this little museum, housed in a renovated 17th-century presbytery. ⓐ rue Xavier d'Authier ⓣ 04 42 01 88 66 ⓛ 10.30–12.30, 15.30–18.30 Wed–Sat

◉ Cassis' brightly coloured townhouses

RETAIL THERAPY

L'Art du Temps Linger over the eclectic choice of painted ceramics, antique restored furniture and Provençal paintings. ⓐ 10 rue Pierre-Eydin ⓣ 04 42 01 88 55 ⓛ 10.00–19.30 Mon–Sat

Maison des Vins If you've fallen in love with the local wines, head to this speciality store to pick up a few bottles. Staying in a self-catering apartment? Pop next door to the Maison des Coquillages for some seafood to have along with your wine. ⓐ route de Marseilles ⓣ 04 42 01 15 61 ⓛ 09.15–12.30, 14.30–19.00 Mon–Fri, 10.00–12.00, 15.00–18.00 Sat & Sun ⓦ www.maisondesvinscassis.com

Quai des Artistes Here you can pick up local arts and crafts, as well as quirky flowers. ⓐ quai Calendal ⓛ 19.00–00.00 July & Aug

TAKING A BREAK

Sucr'E delices £ Here you'll find gourmet pastries with a touch of imagination. Traditional sweet cakes and biscuits are often flavoured with a blend of fruits, herbs and vegetables. ⓐ 4 rue Alexandre Gervais ⓣ 04 42 03 59 79 ⓛ 06.30–13.45, 16.00–19.30 Mon–Sat, 06.30–19.30 Sun

Le Chai Cassidain £–££ Pop into this specialist wine bar for a taste of the best local produce. ⓐ 6 rue Séverin Icard ⓣ 04 42 01 99 80 ⓦ www.lechaicassidain.com ⓛ 09.30–22.30

AFTER DARK

L'Oustau de la Mar £ Nestled among the restaurants that line the port, L'Oustau de la Mar serves up spectacular seafood and

excellent-value three-course menus (€23), as well as daily
specials like filet of sole doused in a raspberry butter. ⓐ 20 quai
des Baux ⓣ 04 42 01 78 22 ⓛ 12.00–14.30, 19.00–22.30 Sat–Wed,
19.00–22.30 Fri, mid-Dec–mid-Nov

Fleurs de Thym ££ Set in the town centre, Fleurs de Thym offers
traditional Provençal cuisine made from seasonal local ingredients,
like red mullet and sardines, or courgettes and aubergines.
ⓐ 5 rue Lamartine ⓣ 04 42 01 23 03 ⓦ www.fleursdethym.com
ⓛ 19.00–22.00 Tues–Sun, Oct–Mar

Nino £££ The Brezzo family have been running this upmarket
restaurant on Cassis' port since 1962. The cuisine is modern
French, and the décor has a nautical theme. The restaurant also
rents *chambres d'hôtes*, rooms in the picturesque buildings
surrounding the port. ⓐ 1 quai Barthelemy ⓣ 04 42 01 74 32
ⓦ www.nino-cassis.com ⓛ 12.00–15.00, 19.00–22.00 Tues–Sun,
mid-Feb–mid-Dec

ACCOMMODATION

Les Cigales £ Just 1.5km (1 mile) outside of Cassis, this ample
campground has 250 sites, and does not accept reservations.
ⓐ av. de la Marne ⓣ 04 42 01 07 34 ⓦ www.campingcassis.com
ⓛ Mid-Mar–mid-Nov

Le Provençal £ The best budget option in Cassis, Le Provençal is
located just steps away from the port. For the enthusiastic hiker,
breakfast (€6.50) can be delivered to the room from 07.00. ⓐ 7 av.
Victor Hugo ⓣ 04 42 01 72 13 ⓦ www.cassis-le-provencal.com

Le Jardin d'Emile ££ The atmosphere is relaxed at this little hotel, just off the plage de Bestouan; the colourful rooms and their adjacent patios are immersed in a lush garden. ⓐ av. de l'Amiral Ganteaume ⓣ 04 42 01 80 55 ⓦ www.lejardindemile.fr

Les Roches Blanches ££ Formerly a 19th-century fortress, the pretty rooms of this hotel look out onto the Calanques and the sea. There is an infinity pool and direct access to the sea. ⓐ route des Calanques ⓣ 04 42 01 09 30 ⓦ www.roches-blanches-cassis.com

THE CALANQUES

SIGHTS & ATTRACTIONS

The best time to visit the Calanques is during the spring and early autumn, avoiding the peaks in temperature that can be reached in this area during the summer months. Note that some Calanques are closed during summer due to the high risk of forest fires – check ⓦ www.calanques.fr for further information.

It takes about 11 hours for an experienced walker to cross the Calanques from Marseilles to Cassis, although there are paths and routes to suit all ability levels. If you are concerned about setting out alone, contact the tourist office who will put you in touch with other hikers heading out together. From Madrague-de-Montredon, it's a relatively easy hike up to the summit of the Massif de Marseilleveyre for expansive views of Marseilles' cityscape. Amble down to the Calanque de Callelongue, where you can catch the bus back to Marseilles. The Calanque de Sormiou is a top spot for rock-climbing (ⓦ www.topo-calanques.com).

It used to be a working fishing port, and the cottages that still surround it are now used as holiday homes. The Calanque de Sugiton is accessible and popular with hikers, and is just over an hour's downhill hike from Luminy. The Calanque d'En Vau may win the prize for most beautiful, with its white sandy beach and turquoise waters. Rent a kayak in Cassis through **Club Sport Loisirs Nautiques** (ⓐ pl. Montmorin ⓣ 04 42 01 80 01) and head here for the day.

If the hiking sounds a little too gruelling, both the peaceful Calanque de Port Pin, with its sandy beach, and the Calanque de Port Miou are within an hour's easy amble from Cassis' town centre. Travelling with young children? Try the Sentier du Petit Prince, a gentle walk around the Cap Cable peninsula. Shuttles run from Cassis' Gorguettes car park.

◆ *Spend an afternoon at one of the area's many beaches*

TAKING A BREAK
Chez Le Belge £ A casual place to stop for salads and abundant plates of pasta, about an hour's hike from Callelongue. ⓐ Calanque de Marseilleveyre ⓣ No telephone, reservations in person only ⓛ 12.00–14.00, 19.00–22.00

AFTER DARK
Le Lunch ££ A beautiful seaside locale in the Calanque de Sormiou. Specialities include *bouillabaisse* and freshly caught fish. Reservations are required, as during the summer months automobile access to this Calanque is restricted. ⓣ 04 91 25 05 37 ⓛ 12.00–14.00, 19.00–21.30 mid-Mar–end Sept ⓘ No credit cards

La Grotte de Callongue ££–£££ All turn-of-the-century French elegance, La Grotte is as famous for its amazing seafood, like the *moules* (mussels), as it is for its long and established history. ⓐ 1 rue Pebrons, Callongue ⓣ 04 91 73 17 79 ⓛ 10.00–01.00

ACCOMMODATION
Auberge de Jeunesse £ The most peaceful spot to bed down for a night in the middle of the Calanques. Sixty dormitory beds are spread over six rooms, and much of the energy comes from solar power. ⓐ La Fontasse ⓣ 04 42 01 02 72 ⓛ Mid-Mar–end Dec

Hôtel Mahogany £££ Try and book one of the 19 sea-facing rooms in this hotel built into a tiny calanque. The private terraces come complete with exquisite views. ⓐ plage du Bestouan ⓣ 04 42 01 05 70 ⓦ www.hotelmahogany.com

Aix-en-Provence

The City of Fountains, Aix-en-Provence was founded in 122 BC, when Sextius Calvinius led the Romans in setting up camp on the site in order to take advantage of the natural hot springs. A mild Provençal town with over 300 sun-dappled days every year, it's no wonder that local boy Cézanne became a world-renowned artist. Visit Aix in June, for the Musique dans la Rue (Music in the Streets) festival, which takes place over the national Fête de la Musique on 21 June, or in the third week of July for the Festival de Aix-en-Provence.

● *Fontaine de la Rotonde, with its sculpture of Justice, Agriculture and the Arts*

GETTING THERE

By rail

Aix-en-Provence is located approximately 30 km (19 miles) from Marseilles. SNCF trains between the two cities run three to four times per hour, from 05.20–23.15 (direction Aix-en-Provence), and from 05.00–21.30 (direction Marseilles). The journey lasts about 50 minutes. For timetables, see ⓦ www.sncf.fr. Aix-en-Provence is also accessible in around three hours by TGV fast train from Paris (ⓦ www.tgv.com). Note that the TGV station is about 12 km (7½ miles) west of the city centre, whereas the SNCF station is located in the centre of town. If you arrive by TGV, hop on one of the shuttle buses which travel to and from

the town centre roughly every 20 minutes between 04.45 and 22.30.

By road

Buses run between Marseilles and Aix every five to ten minutes between 05.50 and 23.50. The *gare routière*, or **bus station** (🅰 av. de l'Europe 📞 08 91 02 40 25 🅦 www.lepilote.com), offers various bus routes to the surrounding towns in Provence.

Departing from Marseilles, if you're driving head to Aix-en-Provence on the A51. Exit at Aix centre. During high season, it's virtually impossible to drive in the city centre or find a place to park on the streets – your best bet is to leave your car at one of the large car parks, such as **Pasteur** (🅰 16 av. Pasteur).

SIGHTS & ATTRACTIONS

Cathédrale Saint-Sauveur

Located on the site of a former Roman temple, this eclectic cathedral was built upon and tweaked over 13 centuries (fifth through to 18th). Note the different architectural styles of the exterior gates, and the three radically different naves (Romanesque, Gothic and baroque). 🅰 34 pl. des Martyrs de la Résistance 📞 04 42 23 45 65

Thermes Sextius

Be like former bathers Pablo Picasso and Winston Churchill and pop into the Sextius Thermal Baths for a day of treatments and relaxation. Be sure to check out the remains of the ancient thermal pool at the entrance. Daily treatments start at €89.

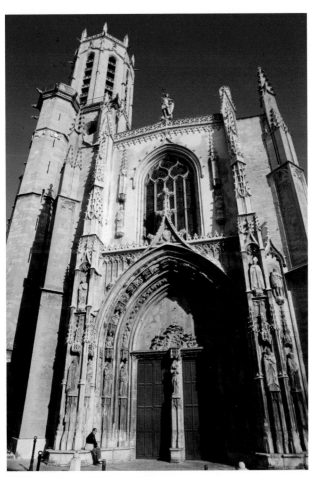

The city's famous Cathédrale Saint-Sauveur

⬥ Mount Sainte-Victoire, just outside Aix, was one of Cézanne's favourite subjects

PAUL CEZANNE

Around these parts, there's no danger of forgetting that Cézanne is Aix's most famous son. Visit the **Aix-en-Provence tourist office** (ⓐ 2 pl. du General de Gaulle ⓣ 04 42 16 11 61 ⓦ www.aixenprovencetourism.com ⓛ 08.30–19.00 Mon–Sat, 10.00–13.00, 14.00–18.00 Sun) to arrange tickets and visits to Jas de Bouffan Manor, the family house purchased by Cézanne's father when the artist was 20, and Cézanne's studio at Les Lauves, which was built to the artist's specifications in 1902. Décor has been arranged as it was upon Cézanne's death. Alternatively, book a day-long **Cézanne Tour** (ⓦ www.atelier-cezanne.com), again through the tourist office.

🅰 55 cours Sextius 🕐 04 42 23 81 82 🅦 www.thermes-sextius.com
🕐 08.30–19.30 Mon–Fri, 08.30–18.30 Sat, 10.30–16.30 Sun

CULTURE

Musée Granet
Located in the 16th-century Priory of the Knights of Malta, the renovated Musée Granet holds an exceptional collection of paintings by French artists during the 17th–19th centuries. There is also a 'Cézanne Room' dedicated to contemplation of nine of the artist's oils, and a small collection of modern art. 🅰 pl. Saint Jean de Malte 🕐 04 42 52 88 32 🅦 www.museegranet-aixenprovence.fr 🕐 11.00–19.00 Tues–Sun, June–Sept; 12.00–18.00 Tues–Sun, Oct–May 🚌 Bus: 4. Admission charge

Musée des Tapisseries (Museum of Tapestries)
Visit an outstanding collection of 17th- and 18th-century tapestries, including the unique 'History of Don Quichotte' tapestry, which dates from 1735. 🅰 Palais de l'Archêveché, 28 pl. des Martyrs de la Résistance 🕐 04 42 23 09 91 🕐 10.00–18.00 Wed–Sun, mid-Apr–mid-Oct; 13.30–17.00 Wed–Sun, mid-Oct–mid-Apr ❶ Closed Jan

RETAIL THERAPY

Genis Be sure to try *calissons*, a sweet speciality of Aix that consists of ground almonds, fruit syrup and a frosted wafer biscuit. Step into old-style Genis to pick up a homemade bag of them. 🅰 1 rue Gaston de Saporta 🕐 04 42 23 30 64 🕐 09.00–19.00

AIX MARKETS

Don't miss the daily **Produce Market** (🕐 08.00–12.30), under the plane trees in place Richelme. Keep an eye out for local producers, who often organise visiting days to their farms (advertised somewhere on their market stall) during key harvest times. Pick up second-hand goods and clothes, as well as fruits and vegetables, at the large market in place des Prêcheurs and place de la Madeleine, with antiques concentrated in **place de Verdun** (🕐 08.00–12.30 Tues, Thur & Sat). Wander through the **Flower Market** (🅐 pl. de l'Hôtel de Ville 🕐 08.00–12.30 Tues, Thur & Sat; 🅐 pl. des Prêcheurs 🕐 08.00–12.30 Wed, Fri, Sun & Mon) to smell the Provençal countryside. During the summer, hit the arts and crafts market in the evening along cours Mirabeau.

🔺 *Early morning at the flower market in Aix*

TAKING A BREAK

Unic Bar £ Go for the €5 breakfast and enjoy the morning action at the local Produce Market. **ⓐ** 40 rue Vauvenargues, on pl. Richelme **ⓣ** 04 42 96 38 28 **ⓛ** 07.00–00.00

Le Café des Deux Garçons ££ Founded in 1792, this café was frequented daily by Cézanne and his good friend Emile Zola, (also from Aix). Stop in for an aperitif on the ample terrace. **ⓐ** 53 cours Mirabeau **ⓣ** 04 42 26 00 51 **ⓛ** 07.00–02.00

AFTER DARK

RESTAURANTS
Geisha Sushi Experience £–££ Linger over outstanding sushi, best enjoyed by candle light on the terrace, next door to Cézanne's father's former hat shop. **ⓐ** 53 cours Mirabeau **ⓣ** 04 42 20 30 00 **ⓛ** 10.00–00.00

Le Zinc d'Hugo £–££ Tucked away from the bustling crowds, this tiny restaurant creates simmering bistro specialities in a cosy atmosphere. This is the perfect spot on a chilly night. **ⓐ** 22 rue Lieutaud **ⓣ** 04 42 27 69 69 **ⓛ** 12.00–14.00, 19.00–22.00 Tues–Sat

Chez Antoine Côté Cour ££ Dine in the plant-filled interior courtyard of Chez Antoine, located just off the cours Mirabeau. The menu blends Italian and Provençal dishes, focusing on seafood and seasonal specialities. **ⓐ** 19 cours Mirabeau **ⓣ** 04 42 93 12 51 **ⓛ** 19.30–22.00 Mon, 12.00–14.00, 19.30–22.00 Tues–Sat

PINK PASSION

Are you crazy about salmon? Head to the **Le Saumon Passion** (££ ⓐ 55 rue Esparit ❶ 04 42 26 73 73 ⓛ 09.00–19.00 Tues–Sat). At this combination deli and tiny restaurant, you can taste pretty much any variety of salmon (Danish, Irish, Norwegian, Baltic...) in any form (wild, marinated, smoked, tarama...) as well as many other types of cured fish and caviar.

Le Clos des Violettes £££ Michelin-starred chef Jean-Marc Banzo whips up exquisite haute cuisine in what is arguably the best restaurant in Aix. Reservations required. ⓐ 10 av. de la Violette ❶ 04 42 23 30 71 ⓦ www.closdelaviolette.com ⓛ 10.00–13.30, 19.00–21.30 Tues–Sat

ACCOMMODATION

Aix offers a wealth of options for accommodation in or near the city. Check the list below, or alternatively, contact the central **Accommodation Booking Office** (ⓐ Office de Tourisme, 2 pl. du General-de-Gaulle, first floor ❶ 04 42 16 11 84 ⓔ resaix@aixenprovencetourism.com) at Aix's tourist office for assistance with direct reservations.

Hôtel Cardinal £ Situated on a sleepy residential road, just across from the Musée Granet, the Hôtel Cardinal's flowery French décor is both elegant and charming. Book a double room, or one of their

six suites, each with kitchenette. ⓐ 24 rue Cardinale ⓣ 04 42 38 32 30
ⓦ www.hotel-cardinal-aix.com

Hôtel de France £ Just around the corner from Aix's central
Rotonde, this little hotel is a bargain spot to bed down for the night.
Walls are a cheery yellow, and temporary art exhibitions are held
on the first floor. Some rooms may be a little on the small side.
ⓐ 63 rue Espariat ⓣ 04 42 27 90 15 ⓦ www.hoteldefrance-aix.com

🔺 *Linger like the locals at one of Aix's many pavement cafés*

Hôtel des Augustins ££ This was formerly a seventh-century convent, and Martin Luther chose to stay here for weeks after his excommunication by the Catholic Church. Perfectly located just off the cours Mirabeau, each of the 29 rooms retains many period features, such as original stonework and antique tiles. **ⓐ** 3 rue de la Masse **ⓣ** 04 42 27 28 59 **ⓦ** www.hotel-augustins.com

Aquabella Hôtel ££–£££ With direct access to the ancient Thermes Sextius Roman thermal baths (as well as the sauna, hammam and heated pool), book a self-indulgent weekend at this modern hotel. **ⓐ** 2 rue des Etuves **ⓣ** 04 42 99 15 00 **ⓦ** www.aquabella.fr

Le Pigonnet £££ At the turn of the century, Cézanne painted Mount Sainte-Victoire from the picturesque garden of this Provençal house. Small and utterly luxurious, with clientele to match. **ⓐ** 5 av. du Pigonnet **ⓣ** 04 42 59 02 90 **ⓦ** www.hotelpigonnet.com

▶ *Marseilles is France's largest and most important port*

PRACTICAL
information

Directory

GETTING THERE
By air

Marseilles Provence Airport (see page 48) is the fourth-busiest in France. Twenty-five airlines offer direct flights to almost 100 cities worldwide, including **British Airways** (to London Gatwick Ⓦ www.britishairways.com), **Aerlingus** (to Dublin Ⓦ www.aerlingus.com) and **Air France** (to Paris, Lisbon, Milan, Rome, Tunis and many other destinations Ⓦ www.airfrance.com). It is also possible to fly directly to Montreal with **Air Transat** (Ⓦ www.airtransat.ca). Terminal 2 (MP2) was opened at the end of 2006 to service low-cost carriers, including **Ryanair** (to many smaller UK airports as well as Marrakech and Fez Ⓦ www.ryanair.com) and **easyJet** (to London Gatwick and Bristol Ⓦ www.easyjet.com).

Many people are aware that air travel emits CO_2, which contributes to climate change. You may be interested in the possibility of lessening the environmental impact of your flight through the charity **Climate Care** (Ⓦ www.climatecare.org), which offsets your CO_2 by funding environmental projects around the world.

By rail

Eurostar trains depart for Paris Gare du Nord from London's renovated St Pancras station. Hop on one of the 17 daily high-speed TGV trains direct from Paris, the fastest reaching Marseilles' Gare Saint-Charles in just under three hours. If you're arriving from other cities in Europe, check Ⓦ www.raileurope.com for general rail information, or ⓦ www.voyages-sncf.fr for details regarding train travel in France. The monthly *Thomas Cook European Rail Timetable* has up-to-date schedules for European international and national train services.

Eurostar ⓘ (UK) 08705 186 186 ⓦ www.eurostar.com

Thomas Cook European Rail Timetable ⓘ (UK) 01733 416477, (USA) 1 800 322 3834 ⓦ www.thomascookpublishing.com

🔺 *Upon exiting the Gare Saint-Charles, the city spills below your feet*

By road

Driving from the UK, it will take approximately two days to cover the 1,200 km (720 miles) from London to Marseilles. Head to Paris, and follow the A6, then the A7 to Marseilles. For driving into Marseilles' city centre, see page 49.

Marseilles' main bus station, the *gare routière*, is well connected to most major European cities. For specific information regarding schedules and prices, check:

National Express Ⓦ www.nationalexpress.com
Eurolines Ⓦ www.eurolines.com

By water

Marseilles' commercial port (see page 52) offers frequent ferries to five destinations in Corsica, including Bastia, Calvi, Ajaccio and Porto Vecchio, as well as Porto Torres in Sardinia and Tunis in Tunisia. For information and timetables, check **SNCM Ferries** (❶ 3260 (in France) or 08 25 88 80 88 Ⓦ www.sncm.fr). Prices vary according to season and special offers. Journey times range from approximately 11 to 27 hours.

ENTRY FORMALITIES

Citizens of the European Union must show a passport or national identity card upon entrance into France. Visas are not required for tourists from the UK, Ireland, USA, Canada Australia or New Zealand who plan to remain in France for less than 90 days. For further details, or if you have doubts as to whether you may require a visa, contact the French embassy or consulate closest to your home, or check Ⓦ www.diplomatie.gouv.fr

Residents of the UK, Ireland and other EU countries may bring tobacco and alcohol for personal use into France. Residents of non-EU countries, and EU residents arriving from a non-EU country, may bring in up to 400 cigarettes and 50 cigars or 50g (2 oz) tobacco; two litres (three bottles) of wine and one litre (approx. two pints) of spirits or liqueurs. The full regulations, as well as definitions of goods for personal use, are detailed on ⓦ www.douane.gouv.fr

MONEY

The euro (€) is the official currency in France. €1 = 100 cents. Notes are €5, €10, €20, €50, €100, €200 and €500, while coins are broken down into denominations of €1 and €2, and 1, 2, 5, 10, 20 and 50 cents.

ATM machines can be found at the airport, railway stations, outside most banks and pretty much on every second or third corner in the city centre. Most accept British and international debit and credit cards. To be on the safe side, ensure that your card has a chip and a pin (often required). ATM machines are the quickest and most convenient way to obtain euros. Instructions on use are usually available in English and other major European languages.

Both Visa and MasterCard are widely accepted; American Express is sometimes accepted, although not always. Traveller's cheques have become relatively difficult to cash in recent years, even at banks – seek out a bureau de change (there is one at the airport). Foreign currencies can be cashed at most banks and bureaux de change – you may have to produce your passport or other ID.

HEALTH, SAFETY & CRIME

Marseilles is a relatively safe city. There really aren't any food and drink precautions that need to be taken, other than ensuring you don't consume excessively! Tap water is fine for drinking, although many people prefer bottled mineral water. Health care ranges from adequate to very good, and emergency services are provided to anyone who needs them. If you are a European citizen or permanent resident, be sure to pack your European Health Insurance Card (EHIC) any time you travel – emergency health care in France will be covered, due to reciprocal European agreements. You may be required to pay for care directly, and you will be reimbursed upon arrival in your home country.

The biggest crime risks for tourists tend to be pickpockets and bag-snatchers – keep your valuables out of sight, and purses should

● *Local police are friendly and helpful*

be zipped up and kept snugly against your body. Dimly lit back streets and the area around the train stations should be avoided at night, particularly if you are alone. Single female visitors should expect that they will be invited for coffee by many a stranger throughout the day. Don't be embarrassed to ignore the invitation and simply walk away. Police in uniform patrol all areas of the city, but tend to keep a low profile.

See Emergencies (page 136) for additional information.

Central Police Station ⓐ 2 rue Antoine Becker ⓣ 04 91 39 80 00 ⓛ 24 hrs ⓝ Bus: 49a, 49b

OPENING HOURS

Shops are normally open 10.00–19.00 Monday to Saturday, often with a one- to two-hour break for lunch. Most shops on the city's main streets, however, do not take a lunch break and may stay open later in the evening as well. Banks are open approximately 08.30–12.00, 13.30–17.00 Monday to Friday. Restaurants usually serve lunch 12.30–14.30 and dinner 19.30–22.30, although in the city centre restaurants may also be open later or serve all day. Most museums are closed on Mondays.

TOILETS

There are public toilets in most public spaces, ranging from coin-operated cabins to crowded cubicles in train stations or shopping centres. You will normally have to pay €0.30–0.50 per person to use these toilets. Stop for a coffee and you can use any café's toilet free of charge, although facilities may be basic. In an emergency, most hotels will allow you to use their toilet (if you look desperate enough!).

CHILDREN

Marseilles' centre is chaotic, and it tends to be difficult to spend prolonged periods of time with young children in the city, unless days are peppered with child-friendly breaks and excursions. That said, there's plenty to do with enthusiastic kids and a little imagination. Try heading to one of the city's many parks, like the Parc Borély, the Jardin du Pharo or the Parc Longchamp. In the summer season, visit Les Catalans Beach and the Roucas Blanc beach at the Parc du Prado – both have sandy beaches suitable for children. Museums such as Musée Cantini (see page 81) often stage afternoon courses for children interested in art. If your family's French is up to scratch, visit **La Baleine qui dit 'Vagues'** (ⓐ 50 cours Julien ⓣ 04 91 48 95 60 ⓦ http://labaleinequiditvagues.org ⓝ Metro: 1 to Réformés Canebière) for children's theatre. Alternately, check ⓦ www.ideesdenfants.com, which lists current activities and ideas for children of all ages.

Overall, Marseilles is welcoming to children in restaurants, and all baby products, such as food and nappies, can be purchased in small and large supermarkets.

COMMUNICATIONS
Internet

Most hotels are now equipped with high-speed internet connections, and often have Wi-Fi, or wireless connections, as well. Check post offices and libraries for additional internet points, or visit one of the city's many internet cafés, such as:
Info Café ⓐ 1 quai Rive Neuve ⓣ 04 91 33 74 98 ⓛ 09.00–22.00 Mon–Sat, 14.30–19.30 Sun ⓝ Metro: 1 to Vieux-Port

TELEPHONING FRANCE

The international code for France is +33 and the area code for Marseilles is 4. To call Marseilles from abroad, dial the access code (usually 00) followed by 33 4 and the eight-digit local number. To call Marseilles from within France, dial 04 and then the local number. The prefix 06 refers to a mobile phone.

TELEPHONING ABROAD

Dial 00, followed by your country code (UK 44, Republic of Ireland 353, USA and Canada 1, Australia 61, New Zealand 64, South Africa 27) and then the area code (leaving out the first 'o' if there is one) and the number.

Phone

To make calls on public telephones, buy phone cards (*télécartes*) at *tabacs* (newsagent/tobacconist shops sporting a red diamond sign outside). Note that 0800 numbers are toll-free within France, while numbers that begin simply 08 are often charged at a higher rate than normal. You can receive telephone calls at public phones with a blue bell symbol on them. If you travel to France often, it may be worth purchasing a French SIM card for your mobile (visit any SFr or Orange mobile phone store for options). All European mobile phones should work in France. If you're travelling from overseas, it's worth checking with your local provider before leaving to ensure coverage.

Post

Postal services in France are reliable. Buy stamps at post offices or tobacconist shops (again, look for the red diamond outside). Sometimes it's also possible to buy stamps at the shops that sell postcards, although you may be required to have actually purchased your postcards in that particular shop. Marseilles' main post office is located at ⓐ 1 pl. Hôtel des Postes (Ⓝ Metro: 1 to Colbert) behind the Centre Bourse shopping centre, but additional post offices are found throughout the city. You can post letters and postcards in the yellow post boxes affixed to building walls at regular intervals around Marseilles.

ELECTRICITY

France runs on 220v with two-pin plugs. British appliances will need a simple adaptor, easily obtained at any electrical or hardware store in Marseilles or at the airport during your travels. US and other equipment designed for 110v will need a *transformateur* (transformer).

TRAVELLERS WITH DISABILITIES

Most public spaces and larger hotels are well equipped with access and facilities adapted for visitors with mobility problems. Pavements in the city centre tend to be wide and road crossings are wheelchair-accessible. However all facilities are not standardised, and access can be difficult in narrow back streets and smaller towns outside of Marseilles. Useful organisations for advice and information include:

RADAR The principal UK forum for people with disabilities.
ⓐ 12 City Forum, 250 City Road, London EC1V 8AF Ⓣ (020) 7250 0212
Ⓦ www.radar.org.uk

SATH (Society for Accessible Travel & Hospitality) advises US-based travellers with disabilities. ⓐ 347 Fifth Ave, Suite 610, New York, NY 10016 ⓣ (212) 447 7284 ⓦ www.sath.org

TOURIST INFORMATION

Marseilles' main tourist office is located just behind the Vieux Port, and is well stocked with information, maps and local literature. They also organise guided tours of the city.

Office du Tourisme et des Congrès ⓐ 4 La Canebière
ⓣ 04 91 13 89 00 ⓦ www.marseille-tourisme.com ⓛ 09.00–20.00 Mon–Sat, 10.00–18.00 Sun, July–Sept; 09.00–19.00 Mon–Sat, 10.00–17.00 Sun, Oct–June

The following websites provide additional useful information about Marseilles and the surrounding areas:
ⓦ www.marseille-france.com
ⓦ www.provencetourism.com
ⓦ www.visitprovence.com

BACKGROUND READING

The Count of Monte Cristo by Alexandre Dumas. This, possibly the best-ever story of revenge, is set on the Ile d'If, off the city's coast.
Cyrano de Bergerac by Edmond Rostand. This classic tale shows that, ultimately, the pen is mightier than the nose.
Marius, Fanny, and César by Marcel Pagnol. This trilogy will grab you and immerse you lovingly in Marseilles' culture.

Emergencies

The following are emergency free-call numbers:

Ambulance (SAMU) ❶ 15
Fire Brigade (*Pompiers*) ❶ 18
Police (*Gendarmerie*) ❶ 17
Any emergency if calling from a mobile phone ❶ 112

MEDICAL SERVICES

If you have a medical situation that needs attention urgently, either call one of the emergency numbers below, or visit a hospital emergency room. Don't forget to keep proof of payment, in order to be reimbursed by your insurance when you arrive home.

Emergency doctor ❶ 04 91 52 91 52
Emergency dentist ❶ 04 91 85 39 39
Poison Treatment Centre ❶ 04 91 75 25 25

POLICE

Should you lose your wallet, or if any of your valuables are stolen, go directly to the police station in order to make an official declaration. You may need this document in order to make insurance claims, or to request duplicates of documents.

Central Police Station ⓐ 2 rue Antoine Becker ❶ 04 91 39 80 00
🕐 24 hrs ⊗ Bus: 49a, 49b
Noailles Police Station ⓐ 66 La Canebière ❶ 04 88 77 58 00
⊗ Metro: 2; tram: T1 to Noailles

Lost property

Hoping someone has turned in your missing item? Head to the
Lost and Found ⓐ 41 blvd de Briancon ⓣ 04 91 14 68 97 ⓛ Mon–Fri

EMBASSIES & CONSULATES

Australia ⓐ 4 rue Jean Rey, Paris ⓣ 01 40 59 33 00
ⓦ www.france.embassy.gov.au
Canada ⓐ 35 av. Montaigne, Paris ⓣ 01 44 43 29 00
ⓦ www.international.gc.ca
New Zealand ⓐ 7 rue Léonard da Vinci, Paris ⓣ 01 45 01 43 43
ⓦ www.nzembassy.com
Republic of Ireland ⓐ 4 rue Rude, Paris ⓣ 01 44 17 67 00
ⓦ www.embassyofireland.fr
South Africa ⓐ 59 quai d'Orsay, Paris ⓣ 01 53 59 23 23
ⓦ www.afriquesud.net
UK Consulate General ⓐ 24 av. du Prado, Marseilles ⓣ 04 91 15 72 10
ⓦ www.britishembassy.gov.uk
USA Consulate ⓐ 12 blvd Paul Peytral, Marseilles ⓣ 04 91 54 92 00
ⓦ http://france.usembassy.gov

EMERGENCY PHRASES

Help!   Au secours!   *Or secoors!*

Call the police/fire service/ambulance!
Appelez la police/les pompiers/une ambulance!
Appeley la police/leh pompee-eh/ewn ambulance!

Editorial/project management: Lisa Plumridge
Copy editor: Monica Guy
Layout/DTP: Alison Rayner
Proofreader: Rebecca Hargrove

The publishers would like to thank the following individuals and organisations for supplying their copyright photographs for this book: BigStockPhoto.com (Kushnirov Avraham, page 47; Dan Talson, page 21); euromediterranée.dr, page 15, iStockphoto.com (Guillaume Dubeg, pages 40–1; Benjamin Lazare, pages 8–9; Munic, page 118; Sean Nel, page 117; Bob Randall, page 42; Diane White Rosier, page 45; Fanelie Rosier, page 59; Lee Walton, page 25); Gérald Passédat, J.Fondacci & C.Cres, page 39; Tristan Rutherford, page 79; Marisa Allegra Williams, page 125; Kathryn Tomasetti, all others.

Send your thoughts to
books@thomascook.com

- Found a great bar, club, shop or must-see sight that we don't feature?
- Like to tip us off about any information that needs a little updating?
- Want to tell us what you love about this handy little guidebook and more importantly how we can make it even handier?

Then here's your chance to tell all! Send us ideas, discoveries and recommendations today and then look out for your valuable input in the next edition of this title.

Email the above address (stating the title) or write to:
pocket guides Series Editor, Thomas Cook Publishing, PO Box 227, Coningsby Road, Peterborough PE3 8SB, UK.

WHAT'S IN YOUR GUIDEBOOK?

Independent authors Impartial up-to-date information from our travel experts who meticulously source local knowledge.

Experience Thomas Cook's 165 years in the travel industry and guidebook publishing enriches every word with expertise you can trust.

Travel know-how Thomas Cook has thousands of staff working around the globe, all living and breathing travel.

Editors Travel-publishing professionals, pulling everything together to craft a perfect blend of words, pictures, maps and design.

You, the traveller We deliver a practical, no-nonsense approach to information, geared to how you really use it.

Useful phrases

English	French	*Approx pronunciation*
BASICS		
Yes	Oui	*Wee*
No	Non	*Nawng*
Please	S'il vous plaît	*Sylvooplay*
Thank you	Merci	*Mehrsee*
Hello	Bonjour	*Bawngzhoor*
Goodbye	Au revoir	*Aw revwahr*
Excuse me	Excusez-moi	*Ekskewzeh-mwah*
Sorry	Désolé(e)	*Dehzoleh*
That's okay	Ça va	*Sahr vahr*
I don't speak French	Je ne parle pas français	*Zher ner pahrl pah frahngsay*
Do you speak English?	Parlez-vous anglais?	*Pahrlay-voo ohnglay?*
Good morning	Bonjour	*Bawng-zhoor*
Good afternoon	Bonjour	*Bawng-zhoor*
Good evening	Bonsoir	*Bawng-swah*
Goodnight	Bonne nuit	*Bun nwee*
My name is ...	Je m'appelle ...	*Zher mahpehl ...*
NUMBERS		
One	Un/Une	*Uhn/Oon*
Two	Deux	*Dur*
Three	Trois	*Trwah*
Four	Quatre	*Kahtr*
Five	Cinq	*Sank*
Six	Six	*Seess*
Seven	Sept	*Seht*
Eight	Huit	*Weet*
Nine	Neuf	*Nurf*
Ten	Dix	*Deess*
Twenty	Vingt	*Vang*
Fifty	Cinquante	*Sangkahnt*
One hundred	Cent	*Sohn*
SIGNS & NOTICES		
Airport	Aéroport	*Ahehrohpohr*
Rail station	Gare	*Gahr*
Platform	Quai	*Kay*
Smoking/ No smoking	Permit de fumer/ Interdit de fumer	*Pernhee der foom-eh/ Anterdee der foom-eh*
Toilets	Toilettes	*Twahlaitt*
Ladies/Gentlemen	Femmes/Hommes	*Fam/Ommh*
Subway/Bus	Métro/Bus	*Maytroa/Booss*